Studies in Ada Style

Peter Hibbard
Andy Hisgen
Jonathan Rosenberg
Mary Shaw
Mark Sherman

Studies in Ada Style

Springer-Verlag New York Heidelberg Berlin

Peter Hibbard
Andy Hisgen
Jonathan Rosenberg
Mary Shaw
Mark Sherman

Department of Computer Science
Carnegie-Mellon University
Schenley Park
Pittsburgh, Pa. 15213

Library of Congress Cataloging in Publication Data
Main entry under title:

Studies in Ada style.

  Includes bibliographical references.
  1. Ada (Computer program language) I. Hibbard,
Peter.
QA76.73.A35S88   001.64'24   81-9323
                                   AACR2

This research was sponsored by the National Science Foundation under
Grant MCS77-03883 and by the Defense Advanced Research Projects
Agency (DOD), ARPA Order No. 3597, monitored by the Air Force
Avionics Laboratory Under Contract F33615-78-C-1551.
The views and conclusions contained in this document are those of the
authors and should not be interpreted as representing the official policies,
either expressed or implied, of the National Science Foundation, the
Defense Advanced Research Projects Agency, or the US Government.

Printed in the United States of America.

9 8 7 6 5 4 3 2 1

ISBN 0-387-**90628-2** Springer-Verlag New York Heidelberg Berlin
ISBN 3-540-**90628-2** Springer-Verlag Berlin Heidelberg New York

Table of Contents

List of Figures

Introduction

The major problems of modern software involve finding effective techniques and tools for organizing and maintaining large, complex programs. The key concept in modern programming for controlling complexity is *abstraction*; that is, selective emphasis on detail. This monograph discusses how the Ada programming language provides ways to support and exploit such abstraction techniques.

The monograph is organized into two parts. The first part traces the important ideas of modern programming languages to their roots in the languages of the past decade and shows how modern languages, such as Ada, respond to contemporary problems in software development.

The second part examines five problems to be programmed using Ada. For each problem, a complete Ada program is given, followed by a discussion of how the Ada language affected various design decisions. These problems were selected to be as practical as possible rather than to illustrate any particular set of language features.

Much of this material has appeared previously in print. An earlier version of the first section, by Mary Shaw, was published as "The Impact of Abstraction Concerns on Modern Programming Languages" in the *Proceedings of the IEEE* special issue on Software Engineering, September 1980, Vol. 68, No. 9, pages 1119-1130. It is reprinted with the IEEE's permission. The article has been updated to reflect the revised Ada syntax and semantics. An earlier version of the second part, by Peter Hibbard, Andy Hisgen, Jonathan Rosenberg and Mark Sherman, was issued as a Carnegie-Mellon Computer Science Department Technical Report CMU-CS-80-149, "Programming in Ada: Examples" (now out of print). Some of the programs have been modified in their use of separate compilation. The commentary on the programs has been expanded and illustrations describing their behavior have been added.

The Impact of Abstraction Concerns on Modern Programming Languages

Mary Shaw

1. The Impact of Abstraction Concerns on Modern Programming Languages

1.1 Issues of Modern Software

The major issues of modern software development stem from the costs of software development, use, and maintenance — which are too high — and the quality of the resulting systems — which is too low. These problems are particularly severe for the large complex programs with long useful lifetimes that characterize modern software. Such programs typically involve many programmers, not only during their development but also for maintenance and enhancement after they are initially released. As a result, the cost and quality of software are influenced by both management and software engineering considerations [7, 28].

This paper examines one of the themes that run through the history of attempts to solve the problems of high cost and low quality: the effect of abstraction techniques and their associated specification and verification issues on the evolution of modern programming languages and methods. This theme places a strong emphasis on engineering concerns, including design, specification, correctness, and reliability.

The paper begins with a review of the ideas about program development and analysis that heavily influenced the development of current techniques (Section 1.2). Many of these ideas are of current interest as well as of historical importance. This review provides a setting for a survey of the ideas from current research projects that are influencing modern language design and software methodology (Section 1.3). Section 1.4 illustrates the changes in program organization that have been stimulated by this work by developing an example in two different languages intended for production use, Ada and Pascal. Although Sections 1.2 and 1.3 present a certain amount of technical detail, Section 1.4 illustrates the concepts with an example that should be accessible to all readers. An assessment of the current status and the potential of current abstraction techniques (Section 1.5) concludes the paper.

1.2 Historical Review of Abstraction Techniques

Controlling software development and maintenance has always involved managing the intellectual complexity of programs and systems of programs. Not only must the systems be created, they must be tested, maintained, and extended. As a result, many different people must understand and modify them at various times during their lifetimes. This section identifies one set of ideas about managing program complexity and shows how those ideas have shaped programming languages and methodologies over the past ten to fifteen years.

A dominant theme in the evolution of methodologies and languages is the development of tools for dealing with abstractions. An *abstraction* is a simplified description, or *specification*, of a system that emphasizes some of the system's details or properties while suppressing others. A *good* abstraction is one in which information that is significant to the reader (i.e., the user) is emphasized while details that are immaterial or diversionary, at least for the moment, are suppressed.

What we call "abstraction" in programming systems corresponds closely to what is called "analytic modelling" in many other fields. It shares many of the same problems: deciding which characteristics of the system are important, what variability (i.e., parameters) should be included, which descriptive formalism to use, how the model can be validated, and so on. As in many other fields, we often define hierarchies of models in which lower-level models provide more detailed explanations for the phenomena that appear in higher-level models. Our models also share the property that the description is sufficiently different from the underlying system to require explicit validation. We refer to the abstract description of a model as its *specification* and to the next lower-level model in the hierarchy as its *implementation*. The validation that the specification is consistent with the implementation is called *verification*. The abstractions we use for software tend to emphasize functional properties of the software, emphasizing *what* results are to be obtained and suppressing details about *how* this is to be achieved.

Many important techniques for program and language organization have been based on the principle of abstraction. These techniques have evolved in step not only with our understanding of programming issues, but also with our ability to use the abstractions as *formal specifications* of the systems they describe. In the 1960's, for example, the important developments in methodology and languages were centered around functions and procedures, which summarize a program segment in terms of a name and a parameter list. At that time, we only knew how to perform syntactic validity checks, and specification techniques reflected this: "specification" meant little more than "procedure header" until late in the decade. By the late 1970's, developments were centered on the design of data structures, specification techniques drew on quite sophisticated techniques of mathematical logic, and programming language semantics were well enough understood to permit formal verification that these programs and specifications were consistent.

Programming languages and methodologies often develop in response to new ideas about how to cope with complexity in programs and systems of programs. As languages evolve to meet these ideas, we reshape our perceptions of the problems and solutions in response to the new experiences. Our sharpened perceptions in turn generate new ideas which feed the evolutionary cycle. This paper explores the routes by which these cyclic advances in methodology and specification have led to current concepts and principles of programming languages.

1.2.1 Early Abstraction Techniques

Prior to the late 1960's, the set of programming topics regarded as important was dominated by the syntax of programming languages, translation techniques, and solutions to specific implementation problems. Thus we saw many papers on solutions to specific problems such as parsing, storage allocation, and data representation. Procedures were well-understood, and libraries of procedures were set up. These libraries met with mixed success, often because the documentation (informal specification) was inadequate or because the parameterization of the procedures did not support the cases of interest. Basic data structures such as stacks and linked lists were just beginning to be understood, but they were sufficiently unfamiliar that it was difficult to separate the concepts from the particular implementations. Perhaps it was too early in the history of the field for generalization and synthesis to take place, but in any event abstraction played only a minor role.

Abstraction was first treated consciously as a program organization technique in the late 1960's. Earlier languages supported built-in data types including at least integers, real numbers, and arrays, and sometimes booleans, high-precision reals, etc. Data structures were first treated systematically in 1968 (the first edition of [50]), and the notion that a programmer might define data types tailored to a particular problem first appeared in 1967 (e.g., [80]).   Although discussions of programming techniques date back to the beginning of the field, the notion that programming is an activity that should be studied and subjected to some sort of discipline dates to the NATO Software Engineering conferences of 1968 [64] and 1969 [9].

1.2.2 Extensible Languages

The late 1960's also saw efforts to abstract from the built-in notations of programming languages in such a way that any programmer could add new notation and new data types to a base language. The objectives of the extensible language work included allowing individual programmers to extend the syntax of the programming language, to define new data structures, to add new operators (including infix operators as well as ordinary functions) for both old and new data structures, and to add new control structures to the base language. This work on extensibility [72] died out, in part because it underestimated the difficulty of defining interesting extensions. The problems included difficulty with keeping independent extensions compatible when all of them modify the syntax of the base language, with organizing definitions so that related information was grouped in common locations, and with finding techniques for describing an extension accurately (other than by exhibiting the code for the extension). However, it left a legacy in its influence on the abstract data types and generic definitions of the 1970's.

1.2.3 Structured Programming

By the early 1970's, a methodology emerged for constructing programs by progressing from a statement of the objective through successively more precise intermediate stages to final code [22, 84]. Called "stepwise refinement" or "top-down programming", this methodology involves approaching a problem by writing a program that is free to assume the existence of any data structures and operations that can be directly applied to the problem at hand, even if those structures and operations are quite sophisticated and difficult to implement. Thus the initial program is presumably small, clear, directly problem-related, and "obviously" correct. Although the assumed structures and operations may be specified only informally, the programmer's intuitions about them should make it possible to concentrate on the overall organization of the program and defer concerns about the implementations of the assumed definitions. When each of the latter definitions is addressed, the same technique is applied again, and the implementations of the high-level operations are substituted for the corresponding invocations. The result is a new, more detailed program that is convincingly like the previous one, but depends on fewer or simpler definitions (and hence is closer to being compilable). Successive steps of the program development add details of the sort more relevant to the programming language than to the problem domain until the program is completely expressed using the operations and data types of the base language, for which a compiler is available.

This separation of concerns between the structures that are used to solve a problem and the way those structures are implemented provides a methodology for decomposing complex problems into smaller, fairly independent segments. The key to the success of the methodology is the degree of abstraction imposed by selecting high-level data structures and operations. The chief limitation of the methodology, which was not appreciated until the methodology had been in use for some time, is that the final program does not preserve the series of abstractions through which it was created, and so the task of modifying the program after it is completed is not necessarily simpler than it would be for a program developed in any other way. Another limitation of the methodology is that informal descriptions of operations do not convey precise information. Misunderstandings about exactly what an operation is supposed to do can complicate the program development process, and informal descriptions of procedures may not be adequate to assure true independence of modules. The development of techniques for formal program specification helps to alleviate this set of problems.

At about the same time as this methodology was emerging, we also began to be concerned about how people understand programs and how programs can be organized to make them easier to understand, and hence to modify. We realized that it is of primary importance to be able to determine what assumptions about the program state are being made at any point in the program. Further, arbitrary transfers of control that span large amounts of program text interfere with this goal. The control flow patterns that lend themselves to understandable programs are the ones that have a single entry point (at the beginning of the text) and, at least conceptually, a single exit point (at the end of the text). Examples of statements that satisfy this rule are the **if...then...else** and the **for** and **while** loops. The chief violator of the rule is the **go to** statement.

The first discussion of this question appeared in 1968 [21], and we converged on a common set of "ideal" control constructs a few years later [22, 42]. Although true consensus on this set of constructs has still not been achieved, the question is no longer regarded as an issue.

1.2.4 Program Verification

In parallel with the development of "ideal" control construct — in fact, as part of their motivation — computer scientists became interested in finding ways to make precise, mathematically manipulatable statements about what a program computes. The ability to make such statements is essential to the development of techniques for reasoning about programs, particularly for techniques that rely on abstract specifications of effects. New techniques were required because procedure headers, even accompanied by prose commentary, provide inadequate information for reasoning precisely about programs, and imprecise statements lead to ambiguities about responsibilities and inadequate separation of modules.

The notion that it is possible to make formal statements about values of variables (a set of values for the variables of a program is called the *program state*) and to reason rigorously about the effect of executing a statement on the program's state first appeared in the late 1960's [24, 39]. The formal statements are expressed as formulas in the predicate calculus, such as

$$y > x \wedge (x > 0 \vee z = x^2).$$

A programming language is described by a set of rules that define the effect each statement has on the logical formula that describes the program state. The rules for the language are applied to the assertions in the program in order to obtain theorems whose proofs assure that the program matches the specification.[1] By the early 1970's the basic concepts of verifying assertions about simple programs and describing a language in such a way that this is possible were under control [42, 57]. When applied by hand, verification techniques tend to be error-prone, and formal specifications, like informal ones, are susceptible to errors of omission [25]. In response to this problem, systems for performing the verification steps automatically have been developed [26]. Verification requires converting a program annotated with logical assertions to logical theorems with the property that the program is correct if and only if the theorems are true. This conversion process, called *verification condition generation*, is well-understood, but considerable work remains to be done on the problem of proving those theorems.

---

[1] A survey of these ideas appears in [56]; introductions to the methods appear in Chapter 3 of [58] and Chapter 5 of [88].

When the emphasis in programming methodology shifted to using data structures as a basis for program organization, corresponding problems arose for specification and verification techniques. The initial efforts addressed the question of what information is useful in a specification [67]. Subsequent attention concentrated on making those specifications more formal and dealing with the verification problems [40]. From this basis, work on verification for abstract data types proceeded as described in Section 1.3.

1.2.5 Abstract Data Types

In the 1970's we recognized the importance of organizing programs into modules in such a way that knowledge about implementation details was localized as much as possible. This led to language support for data types [41], for specifications that are organized using the same structure as data [34, 53, 87], and for generic definitions [73]. The language facilities are based on the **class** construct of Simula [10, 11], ideas about strategies for defining modules [66, 68], and concerns over the impact of locality on program organization [86]. The corresponding specification techniques include strong typing and verification of assertions about functional correctness.

Over the past five years, most research activity in abstraction techniques has been focused on the language and specification issues raised by these considerations; much of the work is identified with the concept of *abstract data types*. Like structured programming, the methodology of abstract data types emphasizes locality of related collections of information. In this case, attention is focused on data rather than on control, and the strategy is to form modules consisting of a data structure and its associated operations. The objective is to treat these modules in the same way as ordinary types such as integers and reals are treated; this requires support for declarations, infix operators, specification of routine parameters, and so on. The result, called an *abstract data type*, effectively extends the set of types available to a program — it explains the properties of a new group of variables by specifying the values one of these variables may have, and it explains the operations that will be permitted on the variables of the new type by giving the effects these operations have on the values of the variables.

In a data type abstraction, we specify the functional properties of a data structure and its operations, then we implement them in terms of existing language constructs (and other data types) and show that the specification is accurate. When we subsequently use the abstraction, we deal with the new type solely in terms of its specification. (This technique is discussed in detail in section 1.3.) This philosophy was developed in several recent language research and development projects, including Ada [16], Alphard [87], CLU [55], Concurrent Pascal [6], Euclid [53], Gypsy [1], Mesa [27] and Modula [85].

The specification techniques used for abstract data types evolved from the predicates used in simple sequential programs. Additional expressive power was incorporated to deal with the way information is packaged into modules and with the problem of abstracting from an implementation to a data type [35]. One class of specification techniques draws on the similarity between a data type and the mathematical structure called an algebra [34, 54]. Another class of techniques explicitly models a newly-defined type by defining its properties in terms of the properties of common, well-understood types [87].

In conjunction with the work on abstract data types and formal specifications, the generic definitions that originated in extensible languages have been developed to a level of expressiveness and precision far beyond the anticipation of their originators. These definitions, discussed in detail in Section 1.3.3, are parameterized not only in terms of variables that can be manipulated during program execution, but also in terms of data types. They can now describe restrictions on which types are acceptable parameters in considerable detail, as in [4].

1.2.6 Interactions Between Abstraction and Specification Techniques

As this review shows, programming languages and methodologies evolve in response to the needs that are perceived by software designers and implementors. However, these perceived needs themselves evolve in response to experience gained with past solutions. The original abstraction techniques of structured programming were procedures or macros[2]; these have evolved to abstract types and generic definitions. Methodologies for program development emerge when we find common useful patterns and try to use them as models; languages evolve to support these methodologies when the models become so common and stable that they are regarded as standard. A more extensive review of the development of software abstractions appears in [32]. As abstraction techniques have become capable of addressing a wider range of program organizations, formal specification techniques have become more precise and have played a more crucial role in the programming process.

For an abstraction to be used effectively, its specification must express all the information needed by the programmer who uses it. Initial attempts at specification used the notation of the programming language to express things that could be checked by the compiler: the name of a routine and the number and types of its parameters. Other facts, such as the description of what the routine computed and under what conditions it should be used, were expressed informally [90]. We have now progressed to the point that we can write precise descriptions of many important relations among routines, including their assumptions about the values of their inputs and the effects they have on the program state. However, many other properties of abstractions are still specified only informally.

---

[2]Although procedures were originally viewed as devices to save code space, they soon came to be regarded, like macros, as abstraction tools.

These include time and space consumption, interactions with special-purpose devices, very complex aggregate behavior, reliability in the face of hardware malfunctions, and many aspects of concurrent processing.   It is reasonable to expect future developments in specification techniques and programming languages to respond to those issues.

The history of programming languages shows a balance between language ideas and formal techniques; in each methodology, the properties we specify are matched to our current ability to validate (verify) the consistency of a specification and its implementation. Thus, since we can rely on formal specifications only to the extent that we are certain that they match their implementations, the development of abstraction techniques, specification techniques, and methods of verifying the consistency of a specification and an implementation must surely proceed hand in hand. In the future, we should expect to see more diversity in the programs that are used as a basis for modularization; we should also expect to see specifications that are concerned with aspects of programs other than the purely functional properties we now consider.

1.3 Abstraction Facilities in Modern Programming Languages

With the historical background of Section 1.2, we now turn to the abstraction methodologies and specification techniques that are currently under development in the programming language research community. Some of the ideas are well enough worked out to be ready for transfer to practical languages, but others are still under development.

Although the ideas behind modern abstraction techniques can be explored independently of programming languages, the instantiation of these ideas in actual languages is also important. Programming languages are our primary notational vehicle for expressing a class of very complex ideas; the concepts we must deal with include not only the functional relations of mathematics, but also constructs that deal with relations over time, such as sequentiality and synchronization. Language designs influence the ways we think about algorithms by making some program structures easier to describe than others. In addition, programming languages are used for communication among people as well as for controlling machines. This role is particularly important in long-lived programs, because a program is in many ways the most practical medium for expressing the structure imposed by the designer — and for maintaining the accuracy of this documentation over time. Thus, even though most programming languages technically have the same expressive power, differences among languages can significantly affect their practical utility.

1.3.1 The New Ideas

Current activity in programming languages is driven by three sets of global concerns: simplicity of design, the potential for applying precise analytic techniques to formal specifications, and the need to control costs over the entire lifetime of a long-lived program.

Simplicity has emerged as a major criterion for evaluating programming language designs. We see a certain tension between the need for "just the right construct" for a task and the need for a language small enough to understand thoroughly. This is an example of a tradeoff between specialization and generality: if highly specialized constructs are provided, individual programs will be smaller, but at the expense of complexity (and feature-by-feature interactions) in the system as a whole. The current trend is to provide a relatively small base language that provides facilities for defining special facilities in a regular way [77]. An emphasis on simplicity underlies a number of design criteria that are now commonly used. When programs are organized to localize information, for example, assumptions shared among program parts and module interfaces can be significantly simplified. The introduction of support for abstract data types in programming languages allows programmers to design special-purpose structures and deal with them in a simple way; it does so by providing a definition facility that allows the extensions to be made in a regular, predictable fashion. The regularity introduced by using these facilities can substantially reduce maintenance problems by making it easier for a programmer who is unfamiliar with the code to understand the assumptions about the program state that are made at a given point in the program — thereby increasing the odds that he or she can make a change without introducing new errors.

Our understanding of the principles underlying programming languages has improved to the point that *formal and quantitative techniques* are both feasible and useful. Current methods for specifying properties of abstract data types and for verifying that those specifications are consistent with the implementation are discussed in Section 1.3.2. Critical studies of testing methods are being performed [44], and interest in quantitative methods for evaluating programs is increasing [70]. It is interesting to note that there seems to be a strong correlation between the ease with which proof rules for language constructs can be written and the ease with which programmers can use those constructs correctly and understand programs that use them.

The 1970's mark the beginning of a real appreciation that the cost of software includes the *costs over the lifetime of the program*, not just the costs of initial development or of execution. For large, long-lived programs, the cost of enhancement and maintenance usually dominate design, development, and execution costs, often by large factors. Two classes of issues arise [18]. First, in order to modify a program successfully, a programmer must be able to determine what other portions of the program depend on the section about to be modified. The problem of making this determination is simplified if the information is localized and if the design structure is retained in the structure of the program. Offline design notes or other documents are not an adequate substitute except in the unlikely case that they are meticulously (and correctly) updated. Second, large programs rarely exist in only one version. The major issues concerning the control of large-scale program development are problems of management, not of programming. Nevertheless, language-related tools can significantly ease the problems. Tools are becoming available for managing the interactions among many versions of a program.

1.3.2 Language Support for Abstract Data Types

Over the past five years, the major thrust of research activity in programming languages and methodology has been to explore the issues related to abstract data types. The current state has emerged directly from the historical roots described in Section 1.2.5. The methodological concerns included the need for information hiding [66, 68] and locality of data access [86], a systematic view of data structures [41], a program organization strategy exemplified by the Simula **class** construct [10, 11], and the notion of generic definition [73]. The formal roots included a proposal for abstracting properties from an implementation [40] and a debate on the philosophy of types, which finally led to the view that types share the formal characteristics of abstract algebras [33, 34, 54, 62].

Whereas structured programming involves progressive development of a program by adding detail to its control structure, programming with abstract data types involves partitioning the program *in advance* into modules that correspond to the major data structures of the final system. The two methodologies are complementary, because the techniques of structured programming may be used within type definition modules, and conversely. An example of the interaction of the two design styles appears in [8].

In most languages that provide the facility, the definition of an abstract data type consists of a program unit that includes the following information:

- *Visible outside the type definition*: the name of the type and the names and routine headers of all operations (procedures and functions) that are permitted to use the representation of the type; some languages also include formal specifications of the values that variables of this type may assume and of the properties of the operations.

- *Not visible outside the type definition*: the representation of the type in terms of built-in data types or other defined types, the bodies of the visible routines, and hidden routines that may be called only from within the module.

An example of a module that defines an abstract data type appears in Figure 1-5.

The general question of abstract data types has been addressed in a number of research projects. These include Alphard [87], CLU [55], Gypsy [1], Russell [14], Concurrent Pascal [6] and Modula [85]. Although they differ in detail, they share the goal of providing language support adequate to the task of abstracting from data structures to abstract data types and allowing those abstract definitions to hold the same status as built-in data types. Detailed descriptions of the differences among these projects are best obtained by studying them in more detail than is appropriate here. As with many research projects, the impact they have is likely to take the form of influence on other languages rather than complete adoption. Indeed, the influence of several of the research projects on Ada [16] and Euclid [53] is apparent.

Programming with abstract data types requires support from the programming language, not simply managerial exhortations about program organization. Suitable language support requires solutions to a number of technical issues involving both design and implementation. These include:

- *Naming*: Scope rules are required to ensure the appropriate visibility of names. In addition, protection mechanisms [48, 63] should be considered in order to guarantee that hidden information remains private. Further, programmers must be prevented from naming the same data in more than one way ("aliasing") if current verification technology is to be relied upon.

- *Type checking*: It is necessary to check actual parameters to routines, preferably during compilation, to be sure they will be acceptable to the routines. The problem is more complex than the type checking problem for conventional languages because new types may be added during the compilation process and the parameterization of types requires subtle decisions in the definition of a useful type checking rule.

- *Specification notation*: The formal specifications of an abstract data type should convey all information needed by the programmer. This is not yet possible, but current progress is described below. As for any specification formalism, it is also necessary to develop a method for verifying that a specification is consistent with its implementation.

- *Distributed properties*: In addition to providing operations that are called as routines or infix operators, abstract data types must often supply definitions to support type-specific interpretation of various constructs of the programming language. These constructs include storage allocation, loops that operate on the elements of a data structure without knowledge of the representation, and synchronization. Some of these have been explored, but many open questions remain [55, 74, 77].

- *Separate compilation*: Abstract data types introduce two new problems to the process of separate compilation. First, type checking should be done across compilation units as well as within units. Second, generic definitions offer significant potential for optimization (or for inefficient implementation).

Specification techniques for abstract data types are the topic of a number of current research projects. Techniques that have been proposed include informal but precise and stylized English [37], models that relate the new type to previously defined types [87], and algebraic axioms that specify new types independently of other types [33]. Many problems remain. The emphasis to date has been on the specification of properties of the code; the correspondence of these specification to informally understood requirements is also important [13]. Further, the work to date has concentrated almost exclusively on the functional properties of the definition without attending, for example, to the performance or reliability.

Not all the language developments include formal specifications as part of the code. For example, Alphard includes language constructs that associate a specification with the implementation of a module; Ada and Mesa expect interface definitions that contain at least enough information to support separate compilation. All the work, however, is based on the premise that the specification must include all information that should be available to a user of the abstract data type. When it has been verified that the implementation performs in accordance with its public specification [40], the abstract specification may safely be used as the definitive source of information about how higher-level programs may correctly use the module. In one sense we build up "bigger" definitions out of "smaller" ones; but because a specification alone suffices for understanding, the new definition is in another sense no bigger than the pre-existing components. It is this regimentation of detail that gives the technique its power.

1.3.3 Generic Definitions

A particularly rich kind of abstract data type definition allows one abstraction to take another abstraction (e.g., a data type) as a parameter. These *generic* definitions provide a dimension of modelling flexibility that conventionally-parameterized definitions lack.

For example, consider the problem of defining data types for an application that uses three kinds of unordered sets: sets of integers, sets of reals, and sets of a user-defined type for points in 3-dimensional space. One alternative would be to write a separate definition for each of these three types. However, that would involve a great deal of duplicated text, since both the specifications and the code will be very similar for all the definitions. In fact, the programs would probably differ only where specific references to the types of set elements are made, and the machine code would probably differ only where operations on set elements (such as the assignment used to store a new value into the data structure) are performed. The obvious drawbacks of this situation include duplicated code, redundant programming effort, and complicated maintenance (since bugs must be fixed and improvements must be made in all versions).

Another alternative would be to separate the properties of unordered sets from the properties of their elements. This is possible because the definition of the sets relies on very few specific properties of the elements — it probably assumes only that ordinary assignment and equality operations for the element type are defined. Under that assumption, it is possible to write a single definition, say

```
    type UnOrderedSet(T: type) is ...
```
that can be used to declare sets with several different types of elements, as in

```
    var
            Counters: UnOrderedSet(integer);
            Timers: UnOrderedSet(integer);
            Sizes: UnOrderedSet(real);
            Places: UnOrderedSet(PointIn3Space);
```

using a syntax appropriate to the language that supports the generic definition facility. The definition of UnOrderedSet would provide operations such as Insert, TestMembership, and so on; the declarations of the variables would instantiate versions of these operations for all relevant element types, and the compiler would determine which of the operations to use at any particular time by inspecting the parameters to the routines.

The flexibility provided by generic definitions is demonstrated by the algorithmic transformation of [4], which automatically converts any solution of one class of problems to a solution of the corresponding problem in a somewhat larger class. This generic definition is notable for the detail and precision with which the assumptions about the generic parameter can be specified.

1.4 Practical Realizations

A number of programming languages provide some or all of the facilities required to support abstract data types. In addition to implementations of research projects, several language efforts have been directed primarily at providing practical implementations. These include Ada [16], Mesa [27], Pascal [47] and Simula [10]. Of these, Pascal currently has the largest user community, and the objective of the Ada development has been to make available a language to support most of the modern ideas about programming. Because of the major roles they play in the programming language community, Pascal and Ada will be discussed in some detail.

The evolution of programming languages through the introduction of abstraction techniques will be illustrated with a small program. The program is presented in Fortran IV to illustrate the state of our understanding in the late 1960's. Revised versions of the program in Pascal and Ada show how abstraction techniques for Ada have evolved.

1.4.1 A Small Example Program

In order to illustrate the effects that modern languages have on program organization and programming style, we will carry a small example through the discussion. This section presents a Fortran program for the example; Pascal and Ada versions are developed in Section 1.4.2 and 1.4.3.

The purpose of the program is to produce the data needed to print an internal telephone list for a division of a small company. A data base containing information about all employees, including their names, divisions, telephone numbers, and salaries is assumed to be available. The program must produce a data structure containing a sorted list of the employees in a selected division and their telephone extensions.

Suitable declarations of the employee data base and the divisional telephone list for the Fortran

```
c           Vectors that contain Employee information
c           Name is in EmpNam (24 chars), Phone is in EmpFon (integer)
c           Salary in in EmpSal (real), Division is in EmpDiv (4 chars)
            integer EmpFon(1000), EmpDiv(1000)
            real EmpSal(1000)
            double precision EmpNam(3,1000)

c           Vectors that contain Phone list information
c           Name is in DivNam (24 chars), Phone is in DivFon (integer)
            integer DivFon(1000)
            double precision DivNam(3,1000)

c           declarations of scalars used in program
            integer StafSz, DivSz, i, j
            integer WhichD
            double precision q
```

Figure 1-1: Declarations for Fortran Version of Telephone List Program

implementation are given in Figure 1-1. A program fragment for constructing the telephone list is given in Figure 1-2.

The employee data base is represented as a set of vectors, one for each unit of information about the employee. The vectors are used "in parallel" as a single data structure — that is, part of the information about the ith employee is stored in the ith element of each vector. Similarly, the telephone list is constructed in two arrays, DivNam for names and DivFon for telephone numbers.

The telephone list is constructed in two stages. First, the data base is scanned for employees whose division (EmpDiv(i)) matches the division desired (WhichD). When a match is found, the name and phone number of the employee are added to the telephone list. Second, the telephone list is sorted using an insertion sort.[3]

There are several important things to notice about this program. First, the data about employees is stored in four arrays, and the relation among these arrays is shown only by the similar naming and the comment with their declarations. Second, the character string for each employee's name must be handled in eight-character segments, and there is no clear indication in either the declarations or the code that character strings are involved.[4] The six-line test that determines whether DivNam(*,i) < DivNam(*,j) could be reduced to three tests if it were changed to a test for less-than-or-equal, but this would make the sort unstable. Third, all the data about employees, including salaries, is easily accessible and modifiable; this is undesirable from an administrative standpoint.

---

[3]This selection is not an endorsement of insertion sorting in general. However, most readers will recognize the algorithm, and the topic of this paper is the evolution of programming languages, not sorting techniques.

[4]Indeed, the implementations of floating point in some versions of Fortran interfere with this type violation. Character strings are dealt with more appropriately in the Fortran77 standard.

```
c          Get data for division WhichD only

           DivSz = 0
           do 200 i = 1,StafSz
               if (EmpDiv(i) .ne. WhichD) go to 200
               DivSz = DivSz + 1
               DivNam(1,DivSz) = EmpNam(1,i)
               DivNam(2,DivSz) = EmpNam(2,i)
               DivNam(3,DivSz) = EmpNam(3,i)
               DivFon(DivSz) = EmpFon(i)
200            continue

c          Sort telephone list

           if (DivSz .eq. 0) go to 210
           do 220 i = 1,DivSz
               do 230 j = i+1,DivSz
                   if (DivNam(1,i) .gt. DivNam(1,j)) go to 240
                   if (DivNam(1,i) .lt. DivNam(1,j)) go to 230
                   if (DivNam(2,i) .gt. DivNam(2,j)) go to 240
                   if (DivNam(2,i) .lt. DivNam(2,j)) go to 230
                   if (DivNam(3,i) .gt. DivNam(3,j)) go to 240
                   go to 230
240                do 250 k = 1,3
                       q = DivNam(k,i)
                       DivNam(k,i) = Divnam(k,j)
250                    DivNam(k,j) = q
                   k = DivFon(i)
                   DivFon(i) = DivFon(j)
                   DivFon(j) = k
230                continue
220            continue
210        continue
```

Figure 1-2: Code for Fortran Version of Telephone List Program

1.4.2 Pascal

Pascal [47] is a simple algebraic language that was designed with three primary objectives. It was to support modern programming development methodology; it was to be a simple enough language to teach to students; and it was to be easy to implement reliably, even on small computers. It has, in general, succeeded in all three respects.

Pascal provides a number of facilities for supporting structured programming. It provides the standard control constructs of structured programming, and a formal definition [42] facilitates verification of Pascal programs. It supports a set of data organization constructs that are suitable for defining abstractions. These include the ability to define a list of arbitrary constants as an *enumerated type*, the ability to define heterogeneous **records** with individually named fields, data types that can be dynamically allocated and referred to by pointers, and the ability to name a data structure as a **type** (though not to bundle up the data structure with a set of operations).

The language has become quite widely used. In addition to serving as a teaching language for undergraduates, it is used as an implementation language for micro-computers [5] and it has been extended to deal with parallel programming [6]. An international standardization effort is currently under way [46].

Pascal is not without its disadvantages. It provides limited support for large programs, lacking separate compilation facilities and block structure other than nested procedures. Type checking does not provide quite as much control over parameter passing as one might wish, and there is no support for the encapsulation of related definitions in such a way that they can be isolated from the remainder of the program. Many of the disadvantages are addressed in extensions, derivative languages, and the standardization effort.

```
type
        String = packed array [1..24] of char;
        ShortString = packed array [1..8] of char;
        EmpRec = record
            Name:String;
            Phone:integer;
            Salary:real;
            Division:ShortString;
            end;
        PhoneRec = record Name:String; Phone:integer; end;

var
        Staff: array [1..1000] of EmpRec;
        Phones: array [1..1000] of PhoneRec;
        StaffSize, DivSize,i,j: integer;
        WhichDiv: char;
        q: PhoneRec;
```

Figure 1-3: Declarations for Pascal Version of Telephone List Program

We can illustrate some of Pascal's characteristics by returning to the program for creating telephone lists. Suitable data structures, including both type definitions and data declarations, are shown in Figure 1-3. A program fragment for constructing the telephone list is given in Figure 1-4.

The declarations open with definitions of four types which are not predefined in Pascal. Two (String and ShortString) are generally useful, and the other two (EmpRec and PhoneRec) were designed for this particular problem.

The definition of String and ShortString as types permits named variables to be treated as single units; operations are performed on an entire string variable, not on individual groups of characters. This abstraction simplifies the program, but more importantly, it allows the programmer to concentrate on the algorithm that uses the strings as names, rather than on keeping track of the individual fragments of a name. The difference between the complexity of the code in Figures 1-2 and 1-4 may not seem large, but when it is compounded over many individual composite structures with different representations, the difference can be large indeed. If Pascal allowed programmer-defined types to accept parameters, a single definition of strings that took the string length as a parameter could replace String and ShortString; Ada does allow this, and the change is made in the Ada program of Section 1.4.3.

```
{ Get data for division WhichDiv only }

DivSize := 0;
for i := 1 to StaffSize do
    if Staff[i].Division = WhichDiv then
        begin
        DivSize := DivSize + 1;
        Phones[DivSize].Name := Staff[i].Name;
        Phones[DivSize].Phone := Staff[i].Phone;
        end;

{ Sort telephone list }

for i := 1 to DivSize do
    for j := i+1 to DivSize do
        if Phones[i].Name > Phones[j].Name then
            begin
            q := Phones[i];
            Phones[i] := Phones[j];
            Phones[j] := q;.
            end;
```

Figure 1-4: Code for Pascal Version of Telephone List Program

The type definitions for EmpRec and PhoneRec abstract from specific data items to the notions "record of information about an employee" and "record of information for a telephone list". Both the employee data base and the telephone list can thus be represented as vectors whose elements are records of the appropriate types.

The declarations of Staff and Phones have the effect of indicating that all the components are related to the same information structure. In addition, the definition is organized as a collection of records, one for each employee — so the primary organization of the data structure is by employee. On the other hand, the data organization of the Fortran program was dominated by the arrays that correspond to the fields, and the employees were secondary.

Just as in the Fortran program, the telephone list is constructed in two stages (Figure 1-4). Note that Pascal's ability to operate on strings and records as single units has substantially simplified the manipulation of names and the interchange step of the sort. Another notable difference between the two programs is in the use of conditional statements. In the Pascal program, the use of if ... **then** statements emphasizes the conditions that will cause the bodies of the **if** statements to be executed. The Fortran **if** statements with **go to**'s, however, describe conditions in which code is *not* to be executed, leaving the reader of the program to compute the conditions that actually correspond to the actions.

It is also worth mentioning that the Pascal program will not execute the body of the sort loop at all if no employees work in division WhichDiv (that is, if DivSize is 0). The body of the corresponding Fortran loop would be executed once in that situation if the loop had not been protected by an explicit test for an empty list. While it would do no harm to execute this particular loop once on an empty list, in general it is necessary to guard Fortran loops against the possibility that the upper bound is less than the lower bound.

1.4.3 Ada

The Ada language is currently being developed under the auspices of the Department of Defense in an attempt to reduce the software costs of embedded computer systems. The project includes components for both a language and a programming support environment. The specific objectives of the Ada development include significantly reducing the number of programming languages that must be learned, supported, and maintained within the Department of Defense. The language design emphasized the goals of high program reliability, low maintenance costs, support for modern programming methodology, and efficiency of compilers and object programs [16, 45].

The Ada language developed through competitive designs constrained by a set of requirements [15]. Revisions to the language were completed in the summer of 1980 and the language reference manual was published in November 1980. Development of the programming environment will continue over the next two years [17]. Since compilers for the language are not yet available, it is too soon to evaluate how well the language meets its goals. However, it is possible to describe the way various features of the language are intended to respond to the abstraction issues raised here.

Although Ada grew out of the Pascal language philosophy, extensive syntactic changes and semantic extensions make it a very different language from Pascal. The major additions include module structures and interface specifications for large-program organizations and separate compilation, encapsulation facilities and generic definitions to support abstract data types, support for parallel processing, and control over low-level implementation issues related to the architecture of object machines.

```
package Employee is
    type PrivStuff is limited private;
    type EmpRec is
        record
            Name: string(1..24);
            Phone: integer;
            PrivPart: PrivStuff;
        end record;
    procedure SetSalary(Who: in out EmpRec; Sal: float);
    function GetSalary(Who: EmpRec) return float;
    procedure SetDiv(Who: in out EmpRec; Div: string(1..8));
    function GetDiv(Who: EmpRec) return string(1..8);
private
    type PrivStuff is
        record
            Salary: float;
            Division: string(1..8);
        end record;
end Employee;
```

Figure 1-5: Ada Package Definition for Employee Records

There are three major abstraction tools in Ada. The **package** is used for encapsulating a set of related definitions and isolating them from the rest of the program. The **type** determines the values a variable (or data structure) may take on and how it can be manipulated. The **generic** definition allows many similar abstractions to be generated from a single template, as described in Section 1.3.3.

The incorporation of many of these ideas into Ada can be illustrated through the example of Section 1.4.1. The data organization of the Pascal program (Figures 1-3 and 1-4) could be carried over almost directly to the Ada program, and the result would use Ada reasonably well. However, Ada provides additional facilities that can be applied to this problem. Recall that neither the Fortran program nor the Pascal program can allow a programmer to access names, telephone numbers, and divisions without also allowing him to access private information, here illustrated by salaries. Ada programs can provide such selected access, and we will extend the previous example to do so.

We now organize the program in three components: a definition of the record for each employee (Figure 1-5), declarations of the data needed by the program (Figure 1-6), and code for construction of the telephone list (Figure 1-7).

The **package** of information about employees whose specification is shown in Figure 1-5 illustrates one of Ada's major additions to our tool kit of abstraction facilities. This definition establishes EmpRec as a data type with a small set of privileged operations. Only the specification of the package is presented here. Ada does not require the package body to accompany the specification (though it must be defined before the program can be executed); moreover, programmers are permitted to rely only on the specifications, not on the body of a package. The specification itself is divided into a visible part (everything from **package** to **private**) and a private part (from **private** to **end**). The private part is intended only to provide information for separate compilation.

```
declare
    use Employee;

    type PhoneRec is
        record
            Name: string(1..24);
            Phone: integer;
        end record;

    Staff: array (1..1000) of EmpRec;
    Phones: array (1..1000) of PhoneRec;
    StaffSize, DivSize, i, j: integer range 1..1000;
    WhichDiv: string(1..8);
    q: PhoneRec;
```

Figure 1-6: Declarations for Ada Version of Telephone List Program

Assume that the policy for using EmpRec's is that the Name and Phone fields are accessible to anyone, that it is permissible for anyone to read but not to write the Division field, and that access to the Salary field and modification of the Division. field are supposed to be done only be authorized programs. Two characteristics of Ada make it possible to establish this policy. First, the scope rules prevent any portion of the program outside a package from accessing any names except the ones listed in the visible part of the specification. In the particular case of the Employee package, this means that the Salary and Division fields of an EmpRec cannot be directly read or written outside the package. Therefore the integrity of the data can be controlled by verifying that the routines that are exported from the package are correct. Presumably the routines SetSalary, GetSalary, SetDiv, and GetDiv perform reads and writes as their names suggest; they might also keep records showing who made changes and when. Second, Ada provides ways to control the visibility of each routine and variable name.

Although the field name PrivPart is exported from the Employee package along with Name and Phone, there is no danger in doing so. An auxiliary type was defined to protect the salary and division information; the declaration

    type PrivStuff **is limited private**;

indicates not only that the content and organization of the data structure are hidden from the user (**private**), but also that all operations on data of type PrivStuff are forbidden except for calls on the routines exported from the package. For **limited private** types, even assignment and comparison for equality are forbidden. Naturally, the code inside the body of the Employee package may manipulate these hidden fields; the purpose of the packaging is to guarantee that *only* the code inside the package body can do so.

```
-- Get data for division WhichDiv only

   DivSize := 0;
   for i in 1..StaffSize loop
       if GetDiv(Staff(i)) = WhichDiv then
           DivSize := DivSize + 1;
           Phones(DivSize) := (Staff(i).Name, Staff(i).Phone);
       end if;
   end loop;

-- Sort telephone list

   for i in 1..DivSize loop
       for j in i+1..DivSize loop
           if Phones(i).Name > Phones(j).Name then
               q := Phones(i);
               Phones(i) := Phones(j);
               Phones(j) := q;
           end if;
       end loop;
   end loop;
```

Figure 1-7: Code for Ada Version of Telephone List Program

The ability to force manipulation of a data structure to be carried out only through a known set of routines is central to the support of abstract data types. It is useful not only in examples such as the one given here, but also for cases in which the representation may change radically from time to time and for cases in which some kind of internal consistency among fields, such as checksums, must be maintained. Support for *secure* computation is not among Ada's goals. It can be achieved in this case, but only through a combination of an extra level of packaging and some management control performed in the subprograms. Even without guarantees about security, however, the packaging of information about how employee data is handled provides a useful structure for the development and maintenance of the program.

The declarations of Figure 1-6 are much like the declarations of the Pascal program. The Employee package is used instead of a simple record, and there are minor syntactic differences between the languages. The clause

    use Employee;

says that all the visible names of the Employee package are available in the current block. Since Ada, unlike Pascal, allows nonprimitive types to take parameters, Name's and Division's are declared as String's of specified length.

In the code of the Ada program itself (Figure 1-7), we assume that visibility rules allow the non-private field names of EmpRecs and the GetDiv function to be used. Ada provides a way to create a complete record value and assign it with a single statement; thus the assignment

```
Phones(DivSize) := (Staff(i).Name, Staff(i).Phone);
```

sets both fields of the PhoneRec at once. Aside from this and minor syntactic distinctions, this program fragment is very much like to the Pascal fragment of Figure 1-4.

1.5 Status and Potential

It is clear that methodologies and analytic techniques based on the principle of abstraction have played a major role in the development of software engineering and that they will continue to do so. In this section we describe the ways our current programming habits are changing to respond to those ideas. We also note some of the limitations of current techniques and how future work may deal with them, and we conclude with some suggestions for further reading on abstraction techniques.

1.5.1 How New Ideas Affect Programming

As techniques such as abstract data types have emerged, they have affected both the overall organization of programs and the style of writing small segments of code.

The new languages will have the most sweeping effects on the techniques we use for the high-level organization of program systems, and hence on the management of design and implementation projects. Modularization features that impose controls on the distribution of variable, routine, and type names can profoundly shape the strategies for decomposing a program into modules. Further, the availability of precise (and enforceable) specifications for module interfaces will influence management of software projects [90]. For example, the requirements document for a large avionics system has already been converted to a precise, if informal, specification [37]. Project organization will also be influenced by the growing availability of support tools for managing multiple modules in multiple versions [61].

The organization and style of the code within modules will also be affected. Section 1.4 shows how the treatment of both control and data changes within a module as the same problem is solved in languages with increasingly powerful abstraction techniques.

The ideas behind the abstract data type methodology are still not entirely validated. Projects using various portions of the methodology — such as design based on data types, but no formal specification, or conversely specification and verification without modularity — have been successful, but a complete demonstration on a large project has not yet been completed [75]. Although complete validation experiments have not been done, some of the initial trials are encouraging. A large, interesting program using data-type organization in a language without encapsulation facilities has been written and largely verified [26], and abstract data types specified via algebraic axioms have proved useful as a design tool [36].

1.5.2 Limitations of Current Abstraction Techniques

Efforts to use abstract data types have also revealed some limitations of the technique. In some cases problems are not comfortably cast as data types, or the necessary functionality is not readily expressed using the specification techniques now available. In other cases, the problem requires a set of definitions that are clearly very similar but cannot be expressed by systematic instantiation or invocation of a data type definition, even using generic definitions.

A number of familiar, well-structured program organizations do not fit well into precisely the abstract data type paradigm. These include, for example, filters and shells in the Unix spirit [49] and interactive programs in which the command syntax dominates the specification. These organizations are unquestionably useful and potentially as well-understood as abstract data types, and there is every reason to believe that similarly precise formal models can be developed. Some of these alternative points of view are already represented in high-level design systems for software [30, 69].

Although facilities for defining routines and modules whose parameters may be generic (i.e., of types that cannot be manipulated in the language) have been developed over the past five years, there has been little exploration of the *generality of generic definitions*. Part of the problem has been lack of facilities for specifying the precise dependence of the definition on its generic parameters. A specific example of a complex generic definition, giving an algorithmic transformation that can be applied to a wide variety of problems, has been written and verified [4].

The language investigations described above, together with other research projects [26, 34, 36, 40, 54, 68], have addressed questions of functional specification in considerable detail. That is, they provide formal notations such as input-output predicates, abstract models, and algebraic axioms for making assertions about the effects that operators have on program values. In many cases, the specifications of a system cannot be reduced to formal assertions; in these cases we resort to testing in order to increase our confidence in the program [30]. In other situations, moreover, a programmer is concerned with properties other than pure functional correctness. Such properties include time and space requirements, memory access patterns, reliability, synchronization, and process independence; these have not been addressed by the data type research. A specification methodology that addresses these properties must have two important characteristics. First, it must be possible for the programmer to make and verify assertions about the properties rather than simply analyzing the program text to derive exact values or complete specifications. This is analogous to our approach to functional specifications — we don't attempt to formally derive the mathematical function defined by a program; rather, we specify certain properties of the computation that are important and must be preserved. Further, it is important to avoid adding a new conceptual framework for each new class of properties. This implies that mechanisms for dealing with new properties should be compatible with the mechanisms already used for functional correctness.

A certain amount of work on formal specifications and verification of extra-functional properties has already been done. Most of it is directed at specific properties rather than at techniques that can be applied to a variety of properties; the results are, nonetheless, interesting. The need to address a variety of requirements in practical real-time systems was vividly demonstrated at the conference on Specifications of Reliable Software [79], most notably by Heninger [37]. Other work includes specifications of security properties [23, 60, 82], reliability [83], performance [71, 76] and communication protocols [29].

1.5.3 Further Reading

This paper has included extensive citations in order to make further information about briefly-discussed topics easy to obtain. The purpose of this section is to identify the books and papers that will be most helpful for general or background reading.

General issues of software development, including both management and implementation issues, are discussed in Brook's very readable book [7]. The philosophy of structured programming and the principles of data organization that underlie the representation issues of abstract data types receive careful technical treatment in [11, 22, 41]. The proceedings of the conference on Specifications of Reliable Software [79] contain papers on both prose descriptions of requirements and mathematical specification of abstractions.

More specific (and more deeply technical) readings include Parnas' seminal paper on information hiding [68], Guttag and Horning's discussion of the use of algebraic axioms as a design tool [36], London's survey of verification techniques [56], and papers on specification techniques including algebraic axioms [33] and abstract models [87].

Programming In Ada: Examples

Peter Hibbard
Andy Hisgen
Jonathan Rosenberg
Mark Sherman

1. Introduction to Example Programs

Ada [16] is a language containing many advanced features not available previously in any widely used programming language. These features include: data abstraction mechanisms (packages, private types, derived types, overloading, user redefinition of operators), explicit parallelism and synchronization (tasks, entries, accept statements), a rich separate compilation facility and a powerful strong-typing mechanism. The use of these facilities allows for highly readable, efficient and maintainable programs. However, techniques and paradigms acquired in previous experience with other programming languages do not necessarily carry over directly into good Ada programming techniques. Indeed, our experience has been that a considerable re-learning effort is required to program comfortably in Ada.

This is *not* an introduction either to Ada or to programming. We have assumed a rather high level of knowledge of revised Ada on the part of the reader. In addition, familiarity with data structures, structured programming practices and parallelism is a prerequisite to understanding this part of the monograph.

In choosing examples for inclusion, we considered the following criteria to be essential:

- The examples should be realistic. The feature provided by an example should be of more than academic interest.[1]

- The examples must be self-contained, complete Ada *compilations*. Portions or excerpts of programs are not acceptable.

- The examples must be small enough to be comprehensible with a reasonable amount of effort.

We did *not* choose the examples in an attempt to cover any predetermined number of language features. The aim of our research is to evolve appropriate methods of programming in Ada, and not to explore language design. We therefore decided to allow the programs themselves to dictate the language features to be displayed.

Five examples have been included. The first example is of a generic package providing two abstractions for queues (FIFO lists). The example shows some aspects involved in attempting to implement a convenient, efficient and transportable library package. Both of the queue types are used in later examples in this report.

---

[1] For example, programs like the sieve of Eratosthenes, for determining prime numbers [51], were ruled out for their lack of extra-academic utility.

A simple directed graph package is displayed in chapter 3. The primary purpose of this generic library package is to provide an iterator facility. The use of the iterator, and alternative graph traversal capabilities are discussed. Some interesting trade-offs involved in information hiding versus ease of use and readability are also described.

The next example is highly machine dependent. It is a console teletype driver for a PDP-11[2]. Representation specifications, interrupt handling and machine-dependent programming are illustrated.

The fourth example, contained in chapter 5, is a package providing a string table creation and search mechanism. Interesting uses of generic packages and parameters are shown. Problems encountered in providing a "protected" mechanism are also described.

Chapter 6 contains the last example. A procedure is given that implements the relaxation method for determining the temperature distribution on a rectangular plate. The algorithm is implemented by a user-specified number of tasks. This is an interesting problem in parallelism and synchronization.

All of the examples have been checked for (compile-time) semantic correctness by a semantic analyzer for revised Ada provided to us by Intermetrics, Inc. [78].

Throughout these examples we have included references to relevant sections of the Ada language reference manual [16]. These references are of the form [§ *section number*].

---

[2]PDP is a registered trademark of the Digital Equipment Corporation.

2. An Implementation of Queues

2.1 Description

One of the most common data structures in programs is the queue, which is used frequently as a buffer between processing elements.

The generic package below provides two kinds of queues: a finite queue for use with sequential programs, and a finite queue for use with multi-tasking programs. Each instantiation of the package requires a type parameter that specifies the type of the queued elements. After instantiation, any number of queues may be declared by using the types Queue and Blocking_Queue.

In addition to the package specifications, the following information applies to the use of the package:

- For a queue variable, Q, the invocation Init_Queue must be made once. This invocation must proceed any use of the Append, Remove, Is_Full, Is_Empty or Destroy_Queue subprograms with queue Q.

- When any queue variable Q is no longer needed, the invocation Destroy_Queue(Q) should be made.

- The MaxQueuedElts discriminant to the queue types represents a minimum performance specification. All implementations of Queue_Package will guarantee that at least MaxQueuedElts number of items can be held in a queue.

The two types of queues have different semantics for the Append and Remove operations. The semantics for type Queue are:

- If the specified queue is empty and a call to Remove is made, the exception Empty_Queue will be raised.

- If the specified queue is full and a call to Append is made, the exception Full_Queue will be raised.

The semantics for type Blocking_Queue are:

- If the specified queue is empty and a call to Remove is made, the calling task will be blocked until a corresponding call to Append is made.

- If the specified queue is full and a call to Append is made, the calling task will be blocked until a corresponding call to Remove has been made.

- All operations provided for type Blocking_Queue are indivisible.

2.2 Implementation

The technique used for the static queue is a simple circular array. It is fully analyzed elsewhere [50].

The technique used for the blocking queue is the same except there is an **accept** statement surrounding each operation to provide mutual exclusion and blocking.

2.3 Program Text

```
generic
    type EltType is private;

package Queue_Package is

    type Queue(MaxQueuedElts : Natural) is limited private;

    procedure Append(Q : in out Queue; E : in EltType);
    procedure Remove(Q : in out Queue; E : out EltType);
    function Is_Empty(Q : in Queue) return Boolean;
    function Is_Full(Q : in Queue) return Boolean;
    procedure Init_Queue(Q : in out Queue);
    procedure Destroy_Queue(Q : in out Queue);

    Full_Queue, Empty_Queue : exception;

    type Blocking_Queue(MaxQueuedElts : Natural) is limited private;

    procedure Append(Q : in out Blocking_Queue; E : in EltType);
    procedure Remove(Q : in out Blocking_Queue; E : out EltType);
    function Is_Empty(Q : in Blocking_Queue) return Boolean;
    function Is_Full(Q : in Blocking_Queue) return Boolean;
    procedure Init_Queue(Q : in out Blocking_Queue);
    procedure Destroy_Queue(Q : in out Blocking_Queue);

    pragma Inline(Is_Empty,Is_Full,Init_Queue,Destroy_Queue);

private

    subtype Non_Negative is Integer range 0..Integer'LAST;

    type Queue(MaxQueuedElts : Natural) is
        record
            FirstElt, LastElt : Non_Negative := 0;
            CurSize : Non_Negative := 0;
            Elements: array(0..MaxQueuedElts) of EltType;
        end record;
```

```ada
      task type Blocking_Queue_Task is
         entry Pass_Discriminants(Queue_Size : in Natural);
         entry Put_Element(E : in EltType);
         entry Get_Element(E : out EltType);
         entry Check_Full(B : out Boolean);
         entry Check_Empty(B : out Boolean);
         entry ShutDown;
      end Blocking_Queue_Task;

      type Blocking_Queue(MaxQueuedElts : Natural) is
         record
            Monitor : Blocking_Queue_Task;
         end record;

end Queue_Package;

--------------------------------------------------------------------

package body Queue_Package is

   pragma Inline(Is_Empty,Is_Full,Init_Queue,Destroy_Queue);

   procedure Append(Q : in out Queue; E : in EltType) is
   begin
      if Q.CurSize = Q.MaxQueuedElts then
         raise Full_Queue;
      else
         Q.CurSize := Q.CurSize + 1;
         Q.LastElt := (Q.LastElt + 1) mod Q.MaxQueuedElts;
         Q.Elements(Q.LastElt) := E;
      end if;
   end Append;

   procedure Remove(Q : in out Queue; E : out EltType) is
   begin
      if Q.CurSize = 0 then
         raise Empty_Queue;
      else
         Q.CurSize := Q.CurSize - 1;
         Q.FirstElt := (Q.FirstElt + 1) mod Q.MaxQueuedElts;
         E := Q.Elements(Q.FirstElt);
      end if;
   end Remove;

   function Is_Full(Q : in Queue) return Boolean is
   begin
      return Q.CurSize = Q.MaxQueuedElts;
   end Is_Full;

   function Is_Empty(Q : in Queue) return Boolean is
   begin
      return Q.CurSize = 0;
   end Is_Empty;
```

```ada
procedure Init_Queue(Q : in out Queue) is
begin
   null;
end Init_Queue;

procedure Destroy_Queue(Q : in out Queue) is
begin
   null;
end Destroy_Queue;

task body Blocking_Queue_Task is
   MaxSize: Natural;
begin
   accept Pass_Discriminants(Queue_Size : in Natural) do
      MaxSize := Queue_Size;
   end Pass_Discriminants;

   declare
      Queued_Elements: Queue(MaxSize);
   begin
      Init_Queue(Queued_Elements);

   Monitor_Operations:
      loop
         select
            when not Is_Full(Queued_Elements) =>
               accept Put_Element(E : in EltType) do
                  Append(Queued_Elements, E);
               end Put_Element;
         or
            when not Is_Empty(Queued_Elements) =>
               accept Get_Element(E : out EltType) do
                  Remove(Queued_Elements, E);
               end Get_Element;
         or
               accept Check_Full(B : out Boolean) do
                  B := Is_Full(Queued_Elements);
               end Check_Full;
         or
               accept Check_Empty(B : out Boolean) do
                  B := Is_Empty(Queued_Elements);
               end Check_Empty;
         or
               accept ShutDown;
               exit Monitor_Operations;
         or
               terminate;
            end select;
         end loop Monitor_Operations;
         Destroy_Queue(Queued_Elements);
   end;
end Blocking_Queue_Task;
```

```
procedure Append(Q : in out Blocking_Queue; E : in EltType) is
begin
   Q.Monitor.Put_Element(E);
end Append;

procedure Remove(Q : in out Blocking_Queue; E : out EltType) is
begin
   Q.Monitor.Get_Element(E);
end Remove;

function Is_Full(Q : in Blocking_Queue) return Boolean is
   Temp : Boolean;
begin
   Q.Monitor.Check_Full(Temp);
   return Temp;
end Is_Full;

function Is_Empty(Q : in Blocking_Queue) return Boolean is
   Temp: Boolean;
begin
   Q.Monitor.Check_Empty(Temp);
   return Temp;
end Is_Empty;

procedure Init_Queue(Q : in out Blocking_Queue) is
begin
   Q.Monitor.Pass_Discriminants(Q.MaxQueuedElts);
end Init_Queue;

procedure Destroy_Queue(Q: in out Blocking_Queue) is
begin
   Q.Monitor.ShutDown;
end Destroy_Queue;

end Queue_Package;
```

2.4 Discussion

The implementation of the type Queue is illustrated in Figure 2-1. The queue package has been instantiated with the type Character. The top illustration shows an abstract queue representation for a queue containing three elements. An equivalent representation using the declared record type is shown in the bottom half of the figure.

2.4.1 Use of Limited Private Types

The ability to declare queues is provided via the limited private types Queue and Blocking_Queue [§ 7.4.2]. The need for the private specification should be clear. The only way the package can guarantee correct operation of the Remove and Append procedures is to prevent the package user

38

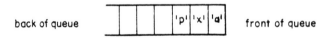

(abstract representation)

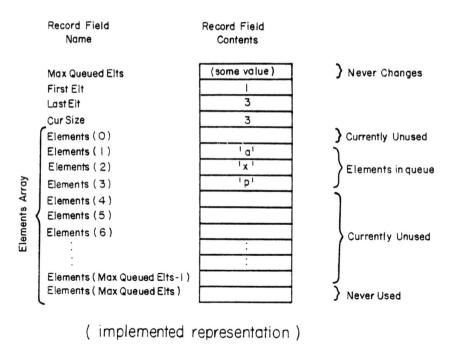

(implemented representation)

Figure 2-1: Implementation of a Queue

from having access to the internal representation. To allow the changing of the queue representation, the package must also guarantee that no part of the user's program depends on the current implementation.

The need to have the type limited is a bit more subtle. Suppose assignment were permitted between two variables of type Queue. After assigning one queue variable to another queue variable, we need to know whether the two variables represent two different queues with the same elements being queued and in the same order, or whether the assignment means that the two variables denote the same queue. In the current implementation, the former semantics would be supported by the assignment statement. If a typical implementation using dynamic storage were provided, the latter interpretation would probably prevail. There are two different meanings for the assignment statement. The equality operator would be even more fuzzy. For example, consider the case where two different queues contained the same elements but happened to be in different array locations in the particular implementation above. Under these conditions, the predefined equality operator would unexpectedly return False. To avoid having the user program depend on one of these interpretations, which could be changed easily, the visible types are both limited and private.

2.4.2 Initialization and Finalization

In the description of this package, we assert that all queues must be initialized by the Init_Queue subprogram. Examination of the package body reveals that the Init_Queue subprogram does nothing for nonblocking queues. It would therefore appear to be unnecessary. However, consider the case where the representation changed from an array to a pointer, and where the implementation used linked list elements with a dummy block at the front of the queue.[3] This representation requires some preprocessing to initialize the data structure before it can be used. To ensure that changing representations is possible, all queue packages provide Init_Queue in their specifications.

Other solutions exist for the initialization problem. For example, it is possible to enclose the data needed for the abstraction in a record along with a boolean variable that indicates if the record has been initialized [§ 3.7]. Default values for record types allow one to guarantee that this boolean variable has the initial value False. Every routine in the package would validate the data structure (by checking the boolean field in the record) before using it. We believe that such an approach is generally wasteful. Many of the clever algorithms for data structure manipulation attempt to avoid extra tests by special features, such as the dummy blocks mentioned above. Requiring a special test before any use of the variable nullifies the added value of many of these algorithms.

Finalization is not as easy to deal with as initialization. The current implementation of nonblocking

---

[3] This technique is discussed in Grogono [31].

queues, as arrays, needs no final processing when the scope containing the queue variable is exited. Exiting from blocks and procedures reclaims the storage automatically. But, suppose the queue's elements were stored in explicitly allocated storage, via **new**. When the scope containing the queue variable is exited, the storage for the queue's elements will remain. By providing a user-level mechanism, such as the Destroy_Queue subprogram, the package assumes the burden of providing a means for releasing unneeded objects.

2.4.3 Passing Tasks as In Out Parameters

Intuition may suggest that the limited private type for Blocking_Queue should be a task type and not a record type. However, there are several advantages to using a record type. If the type had been a task, the only permissible parameter mode for a Blocking_Queue parameter would have been **in** [§ 9.2]. Thus, the specification of the Append procedure would declare the blocking queue parameter as being passed with the **in** mode. This looks very confusing to a programmer working from the package specifications. It is usually assumed that objects that are changed by a subprogram are passed with the **in out** mode. The philosophy of data abstraction in Ada requires that such knowledge be hidden from the user of the package to insure that such knowledge is not exploited in some way. A record may be passed with the **in out** mode, even if the record contains a task type as a component. This technique helps hide the actual implementation.

Furthermore, if the limited private type for Blocking_Queues were a task, user programs could not write subprograms that passed Blocking_Queues as **in out** parameters. This would be a natural way to program as many systems would build subprograms where a queue would be passed along with other data.

There is a third advantage of using a record type rather than a task type. With a record type, the Ada specifications for blocking queues and nonblocking queues are identical. The user could therefore switch from one to the other without having to change other parts of his program (except as it might rely on other parts of the semantics of the queue package).

2.4.4 Passing Discriminants to Tasks

As this example illustrates, it is useful to give parameters to an abstract data type, in this case a queue size specification and an element type. Two methods can be used to accomplish this: a generic parameter can be passed to the package [§ 12.1.1] or a discriminant can be provided for the declared type [§ 3.7.1].

Instantiating the package once for each queue size clutters the program text. Furthermore, it means that each instantiation generates a new queue type and the user would have to duplicate subprograms to handle each size.[4]

Allowing the size of an abstract data type to be part of a subtype is more convenient and familiar to a programmer. This is done by using a discriminant constraint in a record type. Both varieties of queues are therefore implemented with records.

For the blocking queue, there must be a way to pass these discriminant values to the task. This is done by means of the Init_Queue procedure and the Pass_Discriminants entry.

2.4.5 The Elements Array

A close reading of the program reveals that the last element of the Elements array is never used. This results from an interaction between the restrictions on discriminants in Ada and the use of **mod** in the algorithm for calculating index values. The formula for calculating the FirstElt and LastElt values relies on the **mod** function to wrap the index around, from MaxQueuedElts-1 to 0. This avoids a special test necessary when a value is at its maximum and when the algorithm uses array elements 1 through MaxQueuedElts. The rules for discriminants allow only the discriminant to appear as an array bound in a record, not as an expression [§ 3.7.1]. So, MaxQueuedElts must be used instead of MaxQueuedElts-1.

2.4.6 Remove as a Procedure

It might seem natural to have specified Remove as a function instead of as a procedure. We decided that if a queue were to be modified by an operation, it should be passed as an **in out** parameter. However, Ada restricts the modes of parameters to functions to **in** [§ 6.5], therefore we were forced to make Remove a procedure.

---

[4]This is similar to a well known problem in Pascal: arrays with different sizes are different types. This means that one cannot easily write a procedure to sort an arbitrary integer array.

3. A Simple Graph Package Providing an Iterator

3.1 Description

Graphs, of one form or another, are an important data structure throughout most of computer science. This example displays an implementation of a simple package providing an abstraction of directed graphs. The specification includes some type definitions, culminating in the Obj record type, that serves to define the structure of directed graphs. The user is responsible for allocation, initialization and manipulation of the nodes that form a graph.

The primary function of the package is to provide an *iterator* that supplies the means for enabling a user-definable looping abstraction mechanism. This particular iterator provides a facility that may be used to traverse a graph breadth-first.

One might expect that a complete library graph package would provide a much healthier range of functionality than our example does. In addition, it would seem advisable to hide much of the detail that is currently exposed. The package could provide a uniform, implementation-independent manner of creating, manipulating and destroying nodes. We avoided such an implementation, however, to allow the reader an unobstructed view of the iterator.

The algorithm for the breadth-first traversal is a modified version of that in Horwitz and Sahni, page 264 [43] (see Section 3.4.1 of this paper). Other traversal methods, expressed as iterators, could easily be provided. For example, a depth-first traversal would be a primary candidate.

3.2 Specifications

To use the iterator, one must declare a variable of type Breadth_First. The iterator is initialized by invoking the procedure Start. Start takes three parameters:

B   The iterator to initialize.

N   The node at which the breadth-first traversal is to begin. If N=null, the exception Null_Node is raised and initialization is not completed.

Max_Nodes   The maximum number of nodes which might be reached during this search. A rather generous estimate of this value may be provided with little cost in unnecessary overhead. If this number proves to be insufficient, the exception Too_Many_Nodes will be raised at some point by the Next function (see below).

Due to the algorithm chosen, there is an upper limit on the total number of graph iterations which may be started (whether used to completion or not). If this limit is exceeded, the exception Too_Many_Traversals will be raised (see section 3.4.1).

Once an iterator has been properly initialized, three routines are available:

- The More function may be called to determine if there are reachable nodes which have not yet been generated.

- The next node in the search is obtained via the Next function. For any iterator, B, if More(B)=False, then the invocation Next(B) will raise the exception End_Of_Graph.

- To inform the iterator of the end of its usefulness, the Stop procedure is provided. After invocation, the iterator is available for re-use if desired.

An attempt to invoke More, Next or Stop with an uninitialized iterator will cause the Start_Error exception to be raised. Attempting to Start an iterator more than once, without invoking Stop, will also raise this exception. In addition, only one iterator per package instantiation may be active at any time. Start_Error will be raised if this is violated.

A client of this package should not rely on any semantics which depends on actions taken if edges of a graph are modified during a traversal.

3.3 Program Text

```
-------------------------------------------------------------------
--
-- Directed Graph Package with Iterator
--
-------------------------------------------------------------------

generic
   type Item is limited private;

package Graph_Package is

   type Obj;
   type Node is access Obj;
--
-- The following two type definitions allow a node to have an arbitrary
-- number of descendants.
--
   type Sons_Array is array(Natural range <>) of Node;
   type Sons is access Sons_Array;

   type Hidden_Type is limited private;

   type Obj is
      record
         Contents : Item;
         Descendants : Sons;
         Hidden : Hidden_Type; -- "Hidden" field
      end record;
```

```
--
-- The following specifies the breadth first iterator
--

   type Breadth_First is limited private;

   procedure Start(B : in Breadth_First;
                   N : in Node;
                   Max_Nodes : in Natural);
   function More(B : in Breadth_First) return Boolean;
   function Next(B : in Breadth_First) return Node;
   procedure Stop(B : in Breadth_First);

   Start_Error, Null_Node, End_Of_Graph : exception;
   Too_Many_Traversals, Too_Many_Nodes : exception;

private

   type Hidden_Type is
      record              -- To obtain default initialization
         Counter : Integer := Integer'FIRST;
      end record;

   task type Breadth_First is
      entry Start(N : in Node; Max_Nodes : in Natural);
      entry More(B : out Boolean);
      entry Next(N : out Node);
      entry Stop;
   end Breadth_First;

end Graph_Package;
```

```
    with Queue_Package;           -- From Chapter 2 of this report

package body Graph_Package is

    Start_Flag : Boolean := False;

    Counter : Integer := Integer'FIRST;

-- Counter is incremented by 1 at the start of each traversal.  Each
-- node's Counter field (within Hidden) contains a copy of the value
-- of Counter the last time the node was generated.  Upon reaching a
-- node its Counter field is compared with the variable Counter to
-- determine if it has already been seen during this traversal.

    procedure Start(B : in Breadth_First;
                    N : in Node;
                    Max_Nodes : in Natural) is
    begin
       if Start_Flag then raise Start_Error; end if;
       if N = null then raise Null_Node; end if;
       B.Start(N, Max_Nodes);
       Start_Flag := True;
    end Start;

    function More(B : in Breadth_First) return Boolean is
       Flag : Boolean;
    begin
       if not Start_Flag then raise Start_Error; end if;
       B.More(Flag);
       return Flag;
    end More;

    function Next(B : in Breadth_First) return Node is
       N : Node;
    begin
       if not Start_Flag then raise Start_Error; end if;
       B.Next(N);
       return N;
    end Next;

    procedure Stop(B : in Breadth_First) is
    begin
       if not Start_Flag then raise Start_Error; end if;
       B.Stop;
       Start_Flag := False;
    end Stop;

    task body Breadth_First is separate;

end Graph_Package;
```

```
--------------------------------------------------------------------
--
-- Body of Breadth_First
--
--------------------------------------------------------------------
separate (Graph_Package)

task body  Breadth_First is

   Current : Node;                    -- Node to expand next

   Size : Natural;                    -- This holds a copy of the Max_Nodes
                                      -- parameter to the Start entry.
                                      -- It is necessary because scope of
                                      -- entry parameter is limited to
                                      -- accept body [§ 8.2(h)].

   package Q is new Queue_Package(Node);

   procedure Next_Body(N : out Node; Queue : in out Q.Queue) is separate;

begin

   accept Start(N : in Node; Max_Nodes : in Natural) do
      if Counter = Integer'LAST then
         raise Too_Many_Traversals;
      end if;
      Counter := Counter + 1;
      Current := N;
      N.Hidden.Counter := Counter;
      Size := Max_Nodes;
   end Start;

   declare
      Queue : Q.Queue(Size);
   begin
      Q.Init_Queue(Queue);

   Iterator_Operations:
      loop
         select

            accept More(B : out Boolean) do
               B := Current /= null;
            end More;

         or
            accept Next(N : out Node) do
               Next_Body(N, Queue);
            end Next;
```

```
            or
                accept Stop do
                    Q.Destroy_Queue(Queue);
                end Stop;
                exit Iterator_Operations;

            or
                terminate;   -- Simply die, when scope exited

            end select;
          end loop Iterator_Operations;
      end;

  end Breadth_First;
```

```
--------------------------------------------------------------------
--
-- Body of Next_Body
--
--------------------------------------------------------------------

separate (Graph_Package.Breadth_First)

procedure Next_Body(N : out Node; Queue : in out Q.Queue) is

begin

    if Current = null then
        raise End_Of_Graph;
    end if;

    N := Current;
    if N.Descendants /= null then
        for I in N.Descendants.all'RANGE loop
            declare
                Desc : Node renames N.Descendants(I);
            begin
                if Desc /= null and then Desc.Hidden.Counter < Counter then
                    -- This node has not been seen this traversal
                    Q.Append(Queue, Desc);
                    Desc.Hidden.Counter := Counter;
                end if;
            end;
        end loop;
    end if;

    if Q.Is_Empty(Queue) then
        Current := null;
    else
        Q.Remove(Queue, Current);
    end if;

exception
    when Q.Full_Queue =>
        Start_Flag := False;
        Q.Destroy_Queue(Queue);
        raise Too_Many_Nodes;

end Next_Body;
```

3.4 Discussion

3.4.1 The Algorithm

We chose the particular algorithm for graph traversal because it obviated the need for a "visited" flag in each node. This enabled us to eliminate the associated overhead required to maintain access to all of the flags (to clear them before each traversal).

The representation of graphs is illustrated in Figure 3-1. It shows a five node graph, where each node contains a character. Note that each node is represented by an Obj record. The edges from each node are contained in a separately allocated array of pointers.

The algorithm works by maintaining a single global counter in each iterator and a local counter in each node. The global counter is incremented by one at the beginning of each traversal (initiated by a call to Start). The local counter in a node indicates the value contained in the global counter the last time the node was reached. During a traversal, the local counter of a node may be compared with the global counter to determine if the node was already reached (during this traversal). This node was seen earlier if and only if the local counter is equal to the global counter.

The state of a graph in the midst of an iteration is shown in Figure 3-2. Node A has already been processed, node B has been returned by the last call of Next and nodes C and D have been partially processed by the iteration task. Node E has not been reached by the breadth-first traversal algorithm.

To maintain correctness, when the global counter overflows, we must disallow further traversals. This could be considered a serious restriction on the usefulness of this facility for some compiler implementations. For example, a PDP-11 standard integer is only 16 bits allowing, therefore, only about 64,000 traversals. However, only traversals for the particular package instantiation are affected, since the global counter is allocated on a per-instantiation basis.

A reasonable mechanism for alleviating this problem would be to add a second generic parameter to Graph_Package:

```
generic
    type Item is private;
    type Counter_Type is range <>;
```

The user would supply any Integer type as Counter_Type. The type would be used to declare the global and local counters. This would allow users of implementations which support larger Integer types, such as Long_Integer or Long_Long_Integer, to effect an enormous upper limit on the

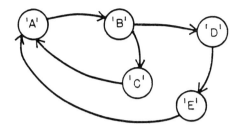

Instantiation was <u>new</u> Graph__Package (Character)

(abstract representation)

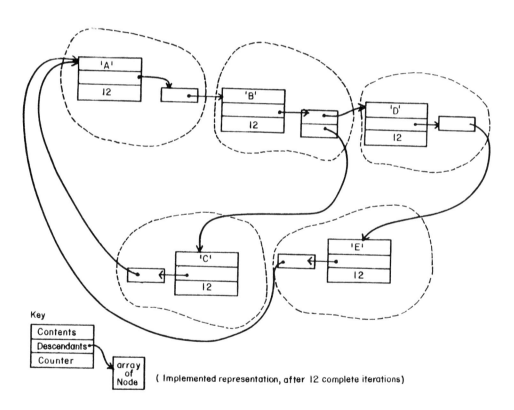

(Implemented representation, after 12 complete iterations)

Figure 3-1: Representation of a Graph

52

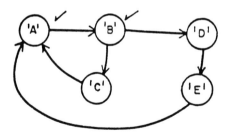

(During the 13th iteration started at node A)
(✓ = visited)
(Currently visiting node B)

(abstract representation)

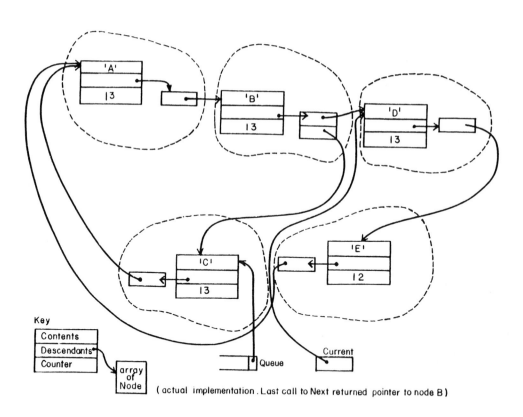

(actual implementation . Last call to Next returned pointer to node B)

Figure 3-2: State of a Graph Traversal

number of traversals.[5]

3.4.2 Information Hiding

Frequently, when designing a package to provide an abstract type, one desires to provide the type with two kinds of structure: a part that is visible to (and, usually, manipulable by) the client, and a part that is hidden from him. This hidden part generally contains data which is specific to the particular implementation. Good programming practice dictates that the user be protected from himself, by not allowing him access to this information. There seems to be no prescribed manner for implementing this in Ada. However, there are several choices available.

The obvious method is to hide *all* of the information from the customer. This is easily accomplished by specifying a (**limited**) **private** type definition for the abstract type [§ 7.4.2]. The disadvantage of this approach is that the package must provide a means for accessing and modifying the "visible" parts of the type structure. This is done most easily by specifying procedures (and, possibly, functions) that perform the actions within the body of the package. Our limited experience indicates that this adds a significant amount of complexity to the specification and use of the abstraction.

For example, the statement

```
X.Contents.Flag := True;
```

might need to be expressed as

```
Temp_Contents := Get_Contents(X);
Temp_Contents.Flag := True;
Set_Contents(X, Temp_Contents);
```

This method does, however, allow a fine degree of control over the abstraction since all access to the objects is strictly controlled.

We believe the scheme we have chosen provides less control but a greater degree of readability than the former scheme.

The idea is to force a form of hiding by placing the desired parts within the public type, but contained within a field whose type is **limited private**. This prevents the user from doing anything significant with the data. Unfortunately, the user can still select the hidden field, as well as declare variables, record fields and formal parameters of this type. Ultimately, however, nothing may be done with these objects.

---

[5] A 36 bit Integer type, as on the PDP-10, would allow for approximately 64 billion traversals. If traversals were initiated at the average rate of 100/second, it would take 20 years to exhaust the capacity of an iterator.

A more serious problem is that the user is not able to perform assignment between objects of the abstract type. This is because it contains a **limited private** field. In contrast, equality for the type may be provided by the package explicitly, if desired.

Admittedly, the solution is imperfect, yet, it provides a form of information hiding intermediate between the previous method and no hiding at all.

3.4.3 In/In Out Parameters

In section 2.4.6, the point was made that parameters that will be modified should probably be passed **in out**. In this specification of Start, Next and Stop we have not followed this policy. We felt that in this case, the readability gained by allowing Next to be a function, outweighed the other considerations. (Recall that functions are not allowed to have **in out** parameters [§ 6.5].)

3.4.4 Using the Iterator

We demonstrate a use of the iterator facility in the following example.

```
    function Reach(From, To : in Node) return Boolean is

        --
        -- Determine if node To is reachable from node From
        --

            B : Breadth_First;

    begin

            Start(B, From, Size);          -- Size is a global
            while More(B) loop
               if Next(B) = To then
                   Stop(B);
                    return True;
                end if;
            end loop;
            Stop(B);
            return False;

        end Reach;
```

Using an alternative loop termination technique, we might replace the body of Reach by

```
      Start(B, From, Size);          -- Size is a global
      loop

          begin
             if Next(B) = To then
                 Stop(B);
                 return True;
             end if;

          exception
             when End_Of_Graph =>
                 Stop(B);
                 return False;
          end;

      end loop;
```

3.4.5 Iterators Versus Generic Procedures

Our decision to provide an iterator is based upon our belief that iterators provide a natural and familiar mechanism for looping. The Ada **for** loop is a simple form of iterator. Several languages, notably IPL-V [65], CLU [55] and Alphard [38, 74], have included user-definable iterator facilities directly in the language definitions.

An alternative to an iterator is to define a generic procedure to enable graph traversal [§ 12.1.3]. Consider the specification

```
      generic
          with procedure Visit(N : in Node; Continue : out Boolean);

      procedure Breadth_First(N : in Node; Max_Nodes : in Natural);
```

To use this facility, the client instantiates Breadth_First with a procedure that performs the desired actions on its Node parameter. The Continue parameter is used to inform the Breadth_First procedure when to stop. Breadth_First would operate by invoking Visit (in reality, the actual procedure parameter instantiated for Visit) once for each node reached. Breadth_First terminates its actions when Continue becomes False.

The procedure Reach, shown previously, might be written

```
function Reach(From, To : in Node) return Boolean is
   Result : Boolean := False;
   procedure Visit(N : in Node; Continue : out Boolean) is
   begin
      if N = To then
         Result := True;
         Continue := False;
      else
         Continue := True;
      end if;
   end Visit;
   procedure Walk is new Breadth_First(Visit);
begin
   Walk(From, Size);                -- Size is a global variable
   return Result;
end Reach;
```

Our primary argument against the generic procedure is that its use obscures the fact that looping is being performed. On the other hand, the iterator provides a facility whose use displays the looping.

3.4.6 Separate Compilation

The graph facility is divided into four compilation units, which must be compiled in the following order: the Graph_Package package specification, the Graph_Package package body, the body of task type Breadth_First and the body of procedure Next_Body. This order is illustrated in Figure 3-3. The decomposition seems to have little advantage for program development; changing the representation of graph nodes would probably require changes in and recompilation of the compilation units.

Part of our motivation for separating the graph facility into multiple compilation units is to improve the readability of the program. For this reason we feel that it is important for the body of Next_Body to be a compilation unit. Ada permits only units declared in the outermost declarative part of a compilation unit to be separately compiled. Had the task body of Breadth_First been present in the body of Graph_Package, the body of Next_Body could not have been separately compiled. The task body of Breadth_First is therefore required to be a compilation unit. Similar situations occur in later examples.

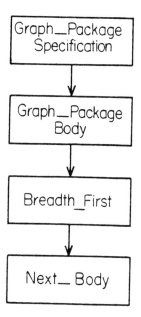

"⟶" means "must be compiled before"

Figure 3-3: Compilation Order for Graph Facility

4. A Console Driver for a PDP-11

4.1 Description

A typical function in embedded systems is performed by a device driver that provides a convenient interface between a system and the particular hardware requirements of an input/output device. Some of the functions performed by this program are buffering of requests for the device, ensuring the integrity and validity of these requests, and fielding interrupts from the hardware.

This example illustrates the general organization that may be used, with some specific details for a PDP-11 console terminal [19, 20].

The device driver program makes the following assumptions about the underlying run-time system and implementation:

- The type that describes the available hardware for the Low_Level_IO package includes the constants Console_Keyboard_Control, Console_Keyboard_Data, Console_Printer_Control, and Console_Printer_Data [§ 14.6]. It is assumed that the system will treat calls of Send_Control and Receive_Control as read and write operations with the correct size and at the correct location (e.g., operations on console devices are mapped into reading and writing locations 777560-777566 octal).

- Specifying a location for an entry means that interrupts using that location will be translated into a call on the entry [§ 13.5.1].

- No data are explicitly passed by an interrupt. All entries that have representation specifications must therefore have no parameters.

In addition to the task specifications, the following information is necessary to use this package:

- The package makes no guarantees about servicing all interrupts. If the underlying run-time system can guarantee that all interrupts will be translated into entry calls, then the package will not lose any interrupts. This says nothing about the proper servicing of those interrupts. On the PDP-11, the datum indicated by an interrupt is lost if the data register of a device is not read before the next interrupt is processed.

- If requests for a device occur faster than the device can process them, the driver will cause the requesting process to block until the request can be processed properly.

- A one-half second delay while waiting for the output device is sufficient time to allow completion of a request. If the output device does not respond within one-half second, the program will initiate the transmission of the next character. Retransmission of characters is not attempted.

- 264 characters of data buffering are provided. The characters passed to the Write_Character procedure will be output without modification.

- The ShutDown entry is used as a way to terminate the device driver cleanly. When a call to ShutDown is made, the currently buffered data will be destroyed. No further processing of these data or servicing of outstanding interrupts will be done by the device driver.

- The Reset entry is functionally equivalent to a ShutDown entry call followed by a re-elaboration of the task declaration. The Reset procedure will also try to send the necessary control signals to reset the hardware device.

Knowledge of the following is also necessary to understand the functioning of this program:

- The device interrupt vectors start at 60 octal for the input device, 64 octal for the output device.

- Device interrupts are enabled by sending the value 100 octal to the device's control register.

4.2 Implementation

A central problem in this example is implementing asynchronous processes with the synchronous mechanism of rendezvous provided by Ada. This is done using three explicit tasks that monitor requests from the program, interrupts from the input device, and interrupts from the output device. All three tasks communicate via shared queues. As long as queues allow fast access, no part of the system will be blocked while waiting for another task to complete a rendezvous. However, if the program produces requests faster than the device can process them, a queue can become full and the requesting task will be blocked.

4.3 Program Text

```
package Terminal_Driver_Package is

    task Terminal_Driver is
        entry Read_Character(C : out Character);
        entry Write_Character(C : in Character);
        entry Reset;
        entry ShutDown;
    end Terminal_Driver;

end Terminal_Driver_Package;
```

```
with Queue_Package, Low_Level_IO;
use Low_Level_IO;

package body Terminal_Driver_Package is

   task body Terminal_Driver is

      -- Group all of the machine dependent constants together

      Console_Input_Vector : constant := 8#60#;
      Console_Output_Vector : constant := 8#64#;
      Enable_Interrupts : Integer := 8#100#;
      Write_Time_Out : constant Duration := 0.5;
      Number_Of_Lines: constant := 2;
      LineLength: constant := 132;

      task type Device_Reader is
         entry Interrupt;
         entry StartUpDone;
         for Interrupt use at Console_Input_Vector;
      end Device_Reader;

      task type Device_Writer is
         entry Interrupt;
         entry StartUpDone;
         for Interrupt use at Console_Output_Vector;
      end Device_Writer;

      package Char_Queue_Package is new Queue_Package(Character);
      use Char_Queue_Package;

      type DriverStateBlock is
         record
            InputCharBuffer, OutputCharBuffer :
               Blocking_Queue(Number_Of_Lines*LineLength);
            CurReader : Device_Reader;
            CurWriter : Device_Writer;
         end record;

      type RefToBlock is access DriverStateBlock;
      CurState: RefToBlock;

      task body Device_Reader is
         TempInput : Character;
      begin
         accept StartUpDone;
         Send_Control(Console_Keyboard_Control, Enable_Interrupts);
         loop
            accept Interrupt do
               Receive_Control(Console_Keyboard_Data, TempInput);
            end Interrupt;
            Append(CurState.InputCharBuffer, TempInput);
         end loop;
      end Device_Reader;
```

```
task body Device_Writer is
   TempOutput : Character;
begin
   accept StartUpDone;
   Send_Control(Console_Printer_Control, Enable_Interrupts);
   accept Interrupt; -- spurious interrupt caused by Send_Control
   loop
      Remove(CurState.OutputCharBuffer, TempOutput);
      Send_Control(Console_Printer_Data, TempOutput);
      select
         accept Interrupt;
      or
         delay Write_Time_Out;
      end select;
   end loop;
end Device_Writer;

procedure ShutDownOld is
begin
   raise CurState.CurReader'FAILURE;
   raise CurState.CurWriter'FAILURE;
   Destroy_Queue(CurState.InputCharBuffer);
   Destroy_Queue(CurState.OutputCharBuffer);
end ShutDownOld;

procedure StartUp is
begin
   CurState := new DriverStateBlock;
   Init_Queue(CurState.InputCharBuffer);
   Init_Queue(CurState.OutputCharBuffer);
   CurState.CurReader.StartUpDone;
   CurState.CurWriter.StartUpDone;
end StartUp;
```

```
    begin
        StartUp;

    Console_Operations:
        loop
            select
                accept Read_Character(C : out Character) do
                    Remove(CurState.InputCharBuffer, C);
                end Read_Character;
            or
                accept Write_Character(C : in Character) do
                    Append(CurState.OutputCharBuffer, C);
                end Write_Character;
            or
                accept Reset do
                    ShutDownOld;
                    StartUp;
                end Reset;
            or
                accept ShutDown;
                ShutDownOld;
                exit Console_Operations;
            or
                terminate;
            end select;
        end loop Console_Operations;
    exception
        when Terminal_Driver'FAILURE =>
            ShutDownOld;

    end Terminal_Driver;

end Terminal_Driver_Package;
```

4.4 Discussion

4.4.1 Use of a Package to Surround the Task

Ada does not allow tasks as library units [§ 10.1]. To allow the inclusion of the Terminal_Driver
task into a library, we have elected to enclose it in a package.

4.4.2 Distinction Between Task Types and Tasks

Unlike most examples of tasks in this report, this task does not explicitly define a type [§ 9.2]. Task
types are usually used when many objects of a particular class are desired. It is probable that only
one driver per physical device is needed. Although it can be argued that a type would allow the use of
the same task type for different terminals (or even devices), the restrictions on address specifications
weakens this argument. The device addresses must be static expressions [§ 13.5]. They cannot be

passed as discriminants to a type (or via an initializing entry call). The only reasonable way to pass these parameters at compile time would be to use generic parameters to the package. Although using generic formal parameters in representation specifications is not prohibited by the current manual [§ 12.1], this limitation is evidently intended. We quote from an official answer from the Ada Joint Program Office:

> The intent is that static expressions should not depend on generic formal parameters, hence a sentence such as the following should be added after the third paragraph after the syntax:
>
> > In addition, if a representation specification requires a static expression, this expression may not depend on a generic formal parameter.[6]

Even if using the generic formal in the representation specification were permitted, the object instantiated would still be a task, not a task type.

There are other reasons for not making .the package generic. A number of parameters would be necessary: four device names, buffering sizes, and time-out values. The use of the device information is also tightly wired into the task. For example, it is known that immediately after enabling interrupts on the output device, a spurious interrupt will be generated that provides no data. This peculiarity may not be true of all devices. Declaring a task type might tempt users to use this driver improperly.

The user may wish to create some higher level operations and capture the terminal driver as part of the representation for some abstract type. Unfortunately, the decision to declare a task instead of a task type prevents the user from using the terminal driver as a component of his type.

4.4.3 Resetting and Terminating the Terminal Driver

Since devices sometimes malfunction, a device driver must be able to deal effectively with this problem. The Ada language intended the FAILURE exception [§ 11.6] and abort statement [§ 9.10] to be used for these purposes, but use of these techniques causes an irreversible exit from the scope of the device driver. By providing the user with additional entries to manipulate the operation of the driver, as well as the operations within the driver, the driver task circumvents this restriction.

---

[6]The Ada Joint Program Office provides a service on the Arpanet for answering technical questions about Ada from groups doing research on the language. The answers to all questions are on the directory <ADA-QUERY> on the Arpanet host USC-ECLB-IPI. This quotation is from the file ANSWERS-12.

4.4.4 Interfacing to Devices

The example shows two design decisions taken to illustrate one possible interface between the hardware and the run-time system for Ada. We have assumed that interrupts are mapped to entries without parameters. We also decided to use Low_Level_IO procedures to access device registers rather than to read or write the (virtual memory) device registers directly.

When a device interrupts the PDP-11, it usually means that a datum can be read from the device's data register. It might seem natural to pass this datum to the entry call mapped to the interrupt. This choice, however, was rejected for three reasons. First, it would require an elaborate explanation of the implementation of entry calls in appendix F of the Language Reference Manual [16]. Entry calls are supposed to be a machine-independent part of the language. The proper place to describe machine dependencies is within the Low_Level_IO package, that is intended to be machine dependent [§ 14.6].

Second, attaching these details to the entry call semantics makes addition of devices more difficult. Each time a new device is added, the compiler must be changed to provide a semantics for it, in particular, the new kind of calling sequence. With the interpretation used in this example, the compiler can translate all entry calls with representation specifications into the same style of code.

Third, it would move the buffering decisions for interrupts from the device driver task to the run-time system. The number of pending interrupts that have not been accepted by a program depends on the amount of buffering the run-time system provides. If input data must also be stored, the number of pending entry calls (from interrupts) is more limited than if no such data were kept. Further, entry call blocks could not be shared between different entries. The decision for this amount of storage would be entirely determined by the run-time system. If only interrupts are handled, the run-time system can optimize its storage to hold only relevant interrupt information. The program can then provide its own buffering for as much or as little data as it desires.

There are cases, such as in radar systems, where the existence of new data immediately invalidates any need to keep old data. Such requirements could not be added easily by the user programmer to the run-time system design. In the case of the console terminal driver, 264 characters of data are buffered. As long as the run-time system will pass on the interrupts faithfully, the package can make claims about the amount of buffering available.

PDP-11 device registers are referenced by reading and writing into designated memory locations. It might seem reasonable to obtain the data in these registers by declaring a variable with a representation specification that maps it to the specified location [§ 13.5]. The decision to use the Low_Level_IO package is motivated by the desire to keep machine dependencies as local as possible. If directly-mapped variables were used, the semantics of the assignment statement and type system would have to define explicitly what is meant when a variable of a certain type is written or read. It is inappropriate to make these decisions just to provide input/output capabilities. For each device that a system supports, it is reasonable and practical to specify exactly the subprograms of Low_Level_IO. Furthermore, as long as these semantics can be guaranteed among different implementations of a machine's architecture, the program can be moved from machine to machine.

5. Table Creation and Table Searching

5.1 Description

In this section we present an example that uses generic packages to provide routines to search a table and to retrieve the items stored there. The table, and auxiliary data objects created to help the search, are encapsulated within a package created by instantiating a generic package. They are not accessible except by the routines exported from that package. A program may have several tables that it can search; a package must be instantiated for each table, and the routines which are exported act specifically upon the table within the corresponding package.

The package has been designed so that the table size is fixed once it has been instantiated. Table look-up returns all items whose keys "match" the given key. A match occurs if the given key is a leading substring of a key associated with an entry. A facility such as this might be used, for example, to store the reserved words for a compiler, or the list of commands available to a command interpreter.

Each entry in the table comprises two parts: a key, implemented as a value of type Text, provided by the library package Text_Handler [§ 7.6], with which the entry will be retrieved, and an item whose type is defined by the user. The generic package Symbol_Table_Package_Generator is instantiated with the item type and the maximum length of a key as parameters, and it yields, among other things, the generic package Symbol_Table. Instantiation of this latter generic package with the table as a parameter causes an auxiliary object to be created to allow fast look-up in the table, and yields functions to search and retrieve entries in the table.

The types provided are:

Entry_Type   The type of each entry in the table.

Table_Type   The type of the table — an array of Entry_Type values.

Table_Pointer This type is private to the package. Values of this type are returned when the table is searched, and they are used to retrieve the entries.

Entry_Collection
          An array of Table_Pointer values.

The functions yielded are:

Make_Entry   This takes a String and an Item_Type and returns a record of type Entry_Type.

Search   This takes a `String` as a parameter. It searches the table and returns an `Entry_Collection` whose elements indicate those entries with keys matching the given key. If no keys match, the `Entry_Collection` returned is a null array. If several keys match, the `Entry_Collection` value has more than one element, and the `Table_Pointers` are sorted by ascending key values.

GetKey   This takes a `Table_Pointer` value and retrieves the key of the element that is indicated.

GetItem   This takes a `Table_Pointer` value and retrieves the item of the element that is indicated.

The exception `Invalid_Table_Pointer` will be raised if `GetItem` or `GetKey` is passed a `Table_Pointer` value that is out of bounds. This might occur if an uninitialized `Table_Pointer` variable were used as a parameter. The exception `MaxSize_Error` will be raised if the size specified for the keys, via the generic parameter `MaxSize`, is too large.

5.2 Implementation

The table of entries passed in as a parameter is not modified by the program. Instead, an auxiliary array of pointers is created and this array is sorted during the elaboration of the package by using a heapsort [52]. Heapsort is preferred over quicksort [52] because it has better behavior if the input table is nearly sorted.

5.3 Program Text

```
-----------------------------------------------------------------
--
-- Generic Package Specifications
--
-----------------------------------------------------------------


with Text_Handler;    -- [§ 7.6]

generic
   type Item_Type is limited private;
   MaxSize : in Natural;

package Symbol_Table_Package_Generator is

   type Entry_Type(Length : Natural) is private;

   function Make_Entry(S : in String;
                       I : in Item_Type) return Entry_Type(MaxSize);

   type Table_Type is array (Integer range <>) of Entry_Type(MaxSize);

   MaxSize_Error : exception;

   generic
      Table : in Table_Type;

   package Symbol_Table is

      type Table_Pointer is private;
      type Entry_Collection is array (Natural range <>) of Table_Pointer;

      function GetKey(Index : in Table_Pointer) return String;
      function GetItem(Index : in Table_Pointer) return Item_Type;
      function Search(Key : in String) return Entry_Collection;

      pragma Inline(GetKey, GetItem);

      Invalid_Table_Pointer : exception;

   private

      type Table_Pointer is new Integer range Table'FIRST..Table'LAST;

   end Symbol_Table;
```

```
private

   type Entry_Type(Length : Natural) is
      record
         Key : Text_Handler.Text(Length);
         Item : Item_Type;
      end record;

end Symbol_Table_Package_Generator;


   ---------------------------------------------------------------
   --
   -- Package Bodies
   --
   ---------------------------------------------------------------

with Text_Handler;

package body Symbol_Table_Package_Generator is

   pragma Inline(GetKey, GetItem);

   function Make_Entry(S : in String;
                       I : in Item_Type) return Entry_Type(MaxSize) is
   begin
      return Entry_Type'(Length => MaxSize,
                         Key => Text_Handler.To_Text(S, MaxSize),
                         Item => I);
   end Make_Entry;

   package body Symbol_Table is separate;

begin          -- Body of Symbol_Table_Package_Generator

   if MaxSize not in Text_Handler.Index then
      raise MaxSize_Error;
   end if;

end Symbol_Table_Package_Generator;
```

```
-----------------------------------------------------------------------
--
-- Body of package Symbol_Table
--
-----------------------------------------------------------------------

separate (Symbol_Table_Package_Generator)

package body Symbol_Table is

    Ptr : Entry_Collection(1..Table'LENGTH);

    L, R, I, J, Reg : Table_Pointer;

    function GetKey(Index : in Table_Pointer) return String is
        -- Returns the key of an entry
    begin
        return Text_Handler.Value(Table(Integer(Index)).Key);
    exception
        when Constraint_Error => raise Invalid_Table_Pointer;
    end;

    function GetItem(Index : in Table_Pointer) return Item_Type is
        -- Returns the item of an entry
    begin
        return Table(Integer(Index)).Item;
    exception
        when Constraint_Error => raise Invalid_Table_Pointer;
    end GetItem;

    function Search(Key : in String) return Entry_Collection is separate;
```

```
begin

-- Initialize ptr

    for Cntr in Ptr'RANGE loop
        Ptr(Cntr) := Table_Pointer(Table'FIRST + Cntr - Ptr'FIRST);
    end loop;

-- Heapsort the table indirectly through Ptr

    L := Ptr'LAST / 2 + 1;
    R := Ptr'LAST;

Outer_Loop:
    loop

        if L > 1 then
            L := L - 1;
            Reg := Ptr(L);
        else
            Reg := Ptr(R);
            Ptr(R) := Ptr(1);
            R := R - 1;
            exit Outer_Loop when R = 1;
        end if;

        J := L;

    Inner_Loop:
        loop
            I := J;
            exit Inner_Loop when J > R/2;
            J := 2 * J;
            if J < R and then GetKey(Ptr(J)) < GetKey(Ptr(J+1)) then
                J := J + 1;
            end if;
            exit Inner_Loop when GetKey(Reg) >= GetKey(Ptr(J));
            Ptr(I) := Ptr(J);
        end loop Inner_Loop;

        Ptr(I) := Reg;

    end loop Outer_Loop;

    Ptr(1) := Reg;

end Symbol_Table;
```

```
------------------------------------------------------------------------
--
-- Body of Search function
--
------------------------------------------------------------------------

separate (Symbol_Table_Package_Generator.Symbol_Table)

function Search(Key : in String) return Entry_Collection is

   -- Search for entries with matching keys

   L, U, Posn, P, Psave, Garbage : Integer;
   Found : Boolean;

   procedure Find(Key : in String;
                  Lower_Bound, Upper_Bound : in Integer;
                  L, U, I : out Integer;
                  Found : out Boolean) is separate;

begin

-- First probe

   Find(Key, Ptr'FIRST, Ptr'LAST, L, U, Posn, Found);

   if U > L then -- Not examined all entries between L and U

      P := Posn;            -- Probe lower region
      loop
         Psave := P;
         Find(Key, L, P-1, L, Garbage, P, Found);
         exit when not Found;
      end loop;
      L := Psave;

      P := Posn;            -- Probe upper region
      loop
         Psave := P;
         Find(Key, P+1, U, Garbage, U, P, Found);
         exit when not Found;
      end loop;
      U := Psave;

   end if;

   return Ptr(L..U);

end Search;
```

```
--------------------------------------------------------------------------
--
-- Body of Find Procedure
--
--------------------------------------------------------------------------

separate (Symbol_Table_Package_Generator.Symbol_Table.Search)

procedure Find(Key : in String;
               Lower_Bound, Upper_Bound : in Integer;
               L, U, I : out Integer;
               Found : out Boolean) is
   -- Binary search
begin
   L := Lower_Bound;
   U := Upper_Bound;

Find_Loop:
   while U >= L loop
      I := (L + U) / 2;
      declare
         Key_Of_Probe : constant String := GetKey(Ptr(I));
      begin
         if Key_Of_Probe'LENGTH > Key'LENGTH then
            exit Find_Loop when
                Key =
                Key_Of_Probe(Key_Of_Probe'FIRST..
                             Key_Of_Probe'FIRST+Key'LENGTH-1);
         else
            exit Find_Loop when Key = Key_Of_Probe;
         end if;
         if Key < Key_Of_Probe then
            U := I - 1;
         else
            L := I + 1;
         end if;
      end;
   end loop Find_Loop;
   Found := U >= L;
end Find;
```

5.4 Discussion

5.4.1 Use of The Package

Following is an example of this package used as part of a command scanner.

```
---------------------------------------------------------------
--
-- Instantiation of the generic packages
--
---------------------------------------------------------------

type Actions is (Find, Delete, Insert, Alter, Execute, Quit);

package Actions_Symbol_Table is
   new Symbol_Table_Package_Generator(Actions, 8);

package My_Symbol_Table is
   new Actions_Symbol_Table.Symbol_Table(
      ( Make_Entry("find", Find),
        Make_Entry("delete", Delete),
        Make_Entry("insert", Insert),
        Make_Entry("enter", Insert),
        Make_Entry("alter", Alter),
        Make_Entry("amend", Alter),
        Make_Entry("execute", Execute),
        Make_Entry("quit", Quit),
        Make_Entry("leave", Quit)
      )
   );
```

5.4.2 Use of the Search Function

The Entry_Collection for the entries with matching keys is found by the following strategy. First a binary search is performed using routine Find. This operates by probing the midpoint of a segment of the table, delimited by L and U, in order to find a match. One of three conditions holds after returning from the call. If L is greater than U then no element matches the given key. If L is equal to U then only one element matches. If L is less than U then the element pointed to by P matches, but there may be other keys between L and U that might also match. To check this, further probes are performed in the lower region delimited by L and P-1, and in the upper region delimited by P+1 and U, using repeated binary searches. The searches are repeated until a call on Find fails to yield a P pointing to a matching key. The value of P yielded by the previous call on Find is the smallest or largest entry in the table that matches the given key.

We illustrate this searching procedure in Figures 5-1, 5-2 and 5-3. Each illustration shows the keys in the table, the values of the input parameters to Find (downward arrows) and the value of the output parameters to Find (upward arrows). The figures trace the calls to Find with the key value "abm".

The first call to Find locates an entry whose key has "abm" as a prefix. The results of this call are shown in Figure 5-1. Next the Search function calls Find to locate the lower limit of the sequence of matching keys. The results of this call are illustrated in Figure 5-2. Another call, not displayed, checks for the lower bound. The boolean value False is returned for the Found parameter, indicating that the previous call found the starting point of the sequence of matching keys.

The Search function then locates the upper limit of the sequence of matching keys. Figure 5-3 illustrates the results of first call to Find for this purpose. A new upper bound for the sequence of matching keys is found, but not all of the matching keys may have been isolated. Another call, which is not illustrated, is made therefore to locate the upper bound. This call returns the boolean value False, indicating that the upper limit has been found. The Search function then returns the designated slice of the symbol table.

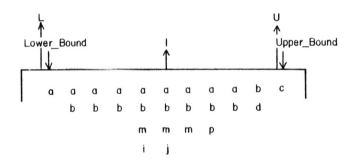

Figure 5-1: Initial Probe into Symbol Table

5.4.3 Use of Packages

This example illustrates several features of the use of generic packages to effect data encapsulation.

- The table is passed into the generic package Symbol_Table as an **in** parameter; thereafter it cannot be manipulated or altered from outside the package [§ 12.1.1]. This assures us that the search function, which relies upon the proper ordering of the keys as established by the initial sort, cannot fail no matter how erroneous is the client program using the package.

- The functions Search, GetItem and GetKey which are exported from a package are specific to the package, and hence to the data encapsulated within it. Thus, it is not necessary to supply further parameters to these functions to indicate which of several tables they are to access. In addition, the type of Table_Pointer is specific to the instance of the package, and therefore it is not possible to access a table in one package with the pointers from some other package.

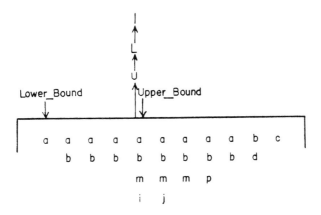

Figure 5-2: Locating Lower Limit of Matches

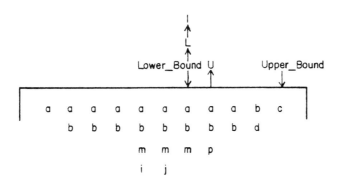

Figure 5-3: Locating Upper Limit of Matches

5.4.4 The Type of the Entries in the Table

In the sorting and searching no use is made of the items in each entry, thus they can be made private to the package; furthermore, by sorting on an auxiliary array of pointers, rather than on the array of entries itself, the package does not require to take copies, and the items can be **limited private**. This has two advantages. First, the item type can be of any size and complexity, without slowing down the sorting, and second, the items can be of any type, including task types.

Choosing an appropriate type for the keys causes some problems. There appear to be three basic choices, none of them entirely satisfactory. In addition to the choice illustrated in the example, we have the following.

- We can implement the key as a String [§ 3.6.3]. The type of the entry then becomes:

```
type Entry_Type(Length : Natural) is
   record
      Key : String(1..Length);
      Item : Item_Type;
   end record;
```

and we must provide a parameter in the first generic instantiation to specify the maximum size of the strings, as in the current example. The aggregate which is then passed as a parameter to the second generic instantiation must contain string literals padded out with the appropriate number of fill characters. This is tedious.

- We could implement the key as an **access** String. The declaration for the Entry_Type then becomes:

```
type Pointer_To_String is access String;

type Entry_Type is
   record
      Key : Pointer_To_String;
      Item : Item_Type;
   end record;

type Table_Type is array (Integer range <>) of Entry_Type;
```

This has the virtue that strings of any size may be used as keys, and no parameter is needed to specify the length (thus the outer generic package will only require the type parameter). Unfortunately, there is a serious flaw in this implementation. Since it is possible for the client to keep an access path to the entries in the table externally to the package, it will be possible to alter the keys. Thus an erroneous client program could alter the behaviour of the package in unpredictable ways.

One additional aspect of these three versions should be mentioned. Only in the case where the key is a String is it possible to create the aggregate at compile time. In the other two cases it will be necessary to create the aggregate at run time, and thus it is likely that two copies of the strings and the items will exist in the memory of the computer. This could preclude the use of the Text_Handler and the **access** String versions if the table is large.

The reader might wonder why the discriminant field Length is present in the record type Entry_Type. This discriminant is used as a discriminant constraint on the Key field of the Entry_Type record. The value of the discriminant is always the same as the generic parameter MaxSize. We are storing unnecessary copies of of the MaxSize constant in the symbol table. We should, it seems, eliminate the discriminant in Entry_Type and use MaxSize to constrain the Key record field. Key is declared with a record type and the manual does not require a non-static discriminant constraint on a record field to be a discriminant of the record. However, recent discussions indicate that this limitation was intended. We quote an official answer from the Ada Joint Program Office:

> The intent is to forbid such "dynamic records" unless there is a dependence on a discriminant. The wording of the manual should be revised accordingly.
>
> A discriminant or index constraint specified for a record component must be static unless it is expressed in terms of a discriminant of the record type itself.[7]

Furthermore, a generic formal parameter cannot be used in other places where a static expression is required, even if the generic actual parameter happens to be static [§ 12.1].

5.4.5 Use of a Private Type for the Pointers to the Table

In order to prevent the user of the package from performing operations on the pointers into the table, and possibly converting a legal pointer into an illegal one, Table_Pointer is made private. There is still the possibility that uninitialized Table_Pointer values will be passed by the client to the routines GetKey and GetItem. The exception Invalid_Table_Pointer is raised if the undefined value happens to violate the range constraints. We could alter the implementation to ensure that all Table_Pointer values are initialized, by making the type be a record type, and by providing initialization [§ 3.7]. We chose not to do it in this example, to avoid further complexity.

5.4.6 Nesting a Generic Package Within a Generic Package

If a package is to have the features we desire, we need at least two generic parameters: the type of the items, and the table that is to be searched. However, the language does not allow us to pass both these parameters at the same time to the same generic package, since the type of the table must be available before we can pass the table as a parameter. Thus it is necessary to have two nested generic packages: the outer takes the type parameter, and produces among other things the type of the table and the inner generic package. The inner package is then instantiated with the table as parameter.

5.4.7 String Comparisons

Several interesting points arise as a result of the need to perform string comparisons within the body of Find [§ 4.5.2]. Several operations need to be performed on the key that is retrieved from the table when it is being probed. Rather than retrieve the key repeatedly, we have decided to take a copy of it and perform the operations on the copy. Since we do not know the size of the string before we retrieve it, we must either take a copy in a new access value, or in a declaration in an inner block. We choose the latter to avoid the need for garbage collection.

---

[7]From file <ADA-QUERY>ANSWER-03 on Arpanet host USC-ECLB-IPI. See footnote on page 64.

5.4.8 Use of Integers in Find

The variables Lower_Bound, Upper_Bound, L, U and I are all declared as Integer, rather than as integers constrained by the bounds of Ptr even though they are used as indexers for Ptr. This is because the algorithm allows them to range from Ptr'FIRST-1 to Ptr'LAST+1. More bounds checking will occur in the body of Find and Search than is necessary, but there is no simple way to avoid this. We considered placing range constraints on the parameters to Find (for example, Lower_Bound, Upper_Bound and P can be constrained to the range 1..Table_Length, and L and U to the range 0..Table_Length+1). While this could help locate errors more accurately, it might also add sufficiently to the complexity of the source that additional errors would be introduced by the programmer.

6. Solution of Laplace's Equation with Several Ada Tasks

6.1 Description

In this section we present the solution of a numerical problem using several Ada tasks. The solution is designed for a multiprocessor computer system such as C.mmp [89] or Cm* [81] in which the processors have access to a shared memory.

Our problem involves the Laplace partial differential equation:[8]

$$\frac{\partial^2 U}{\partial x^2} + \frac{\partial^2 U}{\partial y^2} = 0$$

on a rectangular region D. We are given as boundary conditions the values of U on the edges of D. We are to approximate a solution to the Laplace equation by finding the values of U at each point of a mesh of points in the interior of D. The mesh is an m-by-n rectangular array of points, (i,j), $i = 1,...,m$ and $j = 1,...,n$.

The Laplace equation can be approximated by the difference equations:

$$U_{i+1,j} + U_{i,j+1} + U_{i-1,j} + U_{i,j-1} - 4U_{i,j} = 0$$

The value of U at a point (i,j) is the average of the values of U at the four neighboring points. We have one such equation for each interior point (i,j). Taken together, the equations give us a linear system of simultaneous equations to solve.

Let us number the points (i,j) in row major order, which gives the numbering $1,...,mn$. Let the vector **u** be:

$$\mathbf{u} = (U_1, U_2, ..., U_{mn})$$

Our linear system may then be written as $A\mathbf{u} = 0$. The coefficient matrix, A, is a symmetric band matrix with

- All diagonal elements equal to -4; and

- For non-diagonal elements, $a_{p,q} = 1$ if point p is a neighbor of point q, and 0 otherwise.

The method we will use to solve this system is a parallel version of Gauss-Seidel iteration with N Ada

---

[8] In this presentation, we follow closely the treatment of Dahlquist and Björck [12], sections 5.6 and 8.6.3

tasks.[9] Each task is assigned to work on a portion of the system. Within each portion, the method reduces to the normal single-process Gauss-Seidel iteration. The parallel Gauss-Seidel method was studied by G. Baudet, who implemented it on C.mmp [2, 3].

The Gauss-Seidel iteration formula for deriving the $(n + 1)^{st}$ approximation of $U_{i,j}$ from the nth is:

$$U_{i,j}^{(n + 1)} = (U_{i-1,j}^{(n + 1)} + U_{i,j-1}^{(n + 1)} + U_{i + 1,j}^{(n)} + U_{i,j + 1}^{(n)}) / 4$$

A modification to Gauss-Seidel which accelerates its convergence is the *successive overrelaxation* method. Its iteration formula is:

$$U_{i,j}^{(n + 1)} = U_{i,j}^{(n)} + Omega*(U_{i-1,j}^{(n + 1)} + U_{i,j-1}^{(n + 1)} + U_{i + 1,j}^{(n)} + U_{i,j + 1}^{(n)} - 4U_{i,j}^{(n)}) / 4$$

Here, Omega is the parameter to the successive overrelaxation method.[10] When Omega is equal to 1, the formula reduces to the original Gauss-Seidel formula.

6.2 Implementation

The procedure we provide, `Parallel_Relaxation`, takes the matrix U as a parameter. It is assumed that the outside edge of U has been initialized by the caller with the desired values. The procedure computes the values of U for the interior (i.e., non-edge) points.

In our implementation, the coefficient matrix A is not present explicitly, rather, the coefficients are simply reflected in the iteration formula for successive overrelaxation.

The procedure `Parallel_Relaxation` also takes a parameter, `NumberOfRegions`, which indicates the number of Ada tasks to create. The distribution of pieces of the plate to Ada tasks is illustrated in Figure 6-1.

Each Ada task works on a region of the matrix U. Each region is itself a rectangular matrix. A rectangular grid of such regions is laid out over the interior of the matrix U. One Ada task is dedicated to each region.

Testing for the convergence of the system as a whole must be done with care. To have convergence, each task must believe that its own region has converged, and furthermore, all tasks must hold this belief "simultaneously"; that is, they must reach a unanimous consensus on whether or not they all

---

[9]Besides the treatment of Gauss-Seidel iteration in Dahlquist and Björck [12] and other texts on numerical methods, the reader may wish to refer to McCracken [59], who gives a single-processor treatment of our problem as part of Case Study 11B.

[10]Choosing an appropriate value for Omega is discussed in Dahlquist and Björck [12], sections 5.6 and 8.6.3.

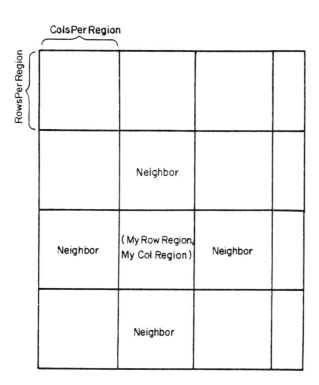

Figure 6-1: Distribution of Tasks

have converged. Observe that a task may decide prematurely that its region has converged, even though a change may soon occur in its region because of a change in one of its neighbors.

For each region task, there is a coordinator task that is used to assist in the communication between the region tasks. The communication consists of one region task, A, advising a neighboring region task, B, that A has not yet converged within its own region. Since A has not yet converged, no conclusion about the convergence of B can be reached, in spite of what B might believe locally. Thus, we can think of this message from A to B as a command to B to keep on going. To avoid deadlock and contention problems which would result if the region tasks did entry calls on each other directly, the message is actually sent by having A do an entry call on B's coordinator task.

The consensus among the region tasks is achieved by passing messages to each other's coordinators, and by having a global counter of the number of unfinished region tasks. When a region task believes that it is done, it decrements the counter. When a coordinator task receives a message that its region could not really be done, it increments the counter. When the counter reaches zero, we know that all region tasks thought they were finished.

Each region task repeatedly executes the following actions. First, it computes one complete new set of values for the points in its region. If the region has not yet converged locally, the task advises its neighbors' coordinators to keep on going. If the region has converged locally, then the task decrements the global counter of unfinished tasks. If the counter is zero, we are done; the task must clean up the system of tasks (described below), and we may then return from the Parallel_Relaxation procedure. If the counter is non-zero, the region task puts itself to sleep by calling an entry of its coordinator, Wait. The coordinator will wake it up by accepting the Wait entry call when a keep-on-going message is received; if such a message had already been received, the coordinator accepts the Wait entry call immediately. The coordinator merges multiple keep-on-going messages that have been received since the last Wait entry call into one message. Multiple keep-on-going messages will thus cause only one acceptance of the Wait entry.

When a region task discovers in the test above that the counter of unfinished region tasks is zero, it must arrange to wake any other region tasks that are sleeping on the Wait entries of their respective coordinators. This must be done because all tasks that are local to a block in Ada must terminate before we may exit the block [§ 9.4]. This waking up is handled by having another entry into the coordinator tasks, the Finish entry. After a Finish entry call is received, a coordinator will immediately accept any Wait entry calls. After a region task returns from the Wait entry call, it looks again to see if the global counter has gone to zero. If it has, the region task concludes that we are done and exits.

Finally, some systems of equations will not converge. As a practical matter, it is important to provide an upper bound on the number of iterations. We do this by having another parameter to `Parallel_Relaxation`, named `MaxIterations`. If this maximum is exceeded, then we set another parameter, `DidNotConverge`, to `True` and return.

6.3 Program Text

6.3.1 A Protected Counter Task Type

Here we present a task type that provides a protected counter with operations for incrementing and decrementing. It is protected in that the increment and decrement operations are indivisible. This indivisibility is achieved by performing the operations within accept bodies [§ 9.5].

We surround the task with a package, so that it may be separately compiled and placed in a library [§ 10.1].

```
package Protected_Counter_Package is

    task type Protected_Counter is
        entry Initialize(Z : in Integer);
        entry Incr(Z : in Integer := 1);
        entry Decr(Z : in Integer := 1);
        entry Read(Z : out Integer);
    end Protected_Counter;

end Protected_Counter_Package;

package body Protected_Counter_Package is

    task body Protected_Counter is
        Counter: Integer;
    begin
        accept Initialize(Z : in Integer) do
            Counter := Z;
        end;

        loop
            select
                accept Incr(Z : in Integer := 1) do
                    Counter := Counter + Z;
                end;
            or
                accept Decr(Z : in Integer := 1) do
                    Counter := Counter - Z;
                end;
            or
                accept Read(Z : out Integer) do
                    Z := Counter;
                end;
            or
                terminate;
            end select;
        end loop;
    end Protected_Counter;

end Protected_Counter_Package;
```

6.3.2 Parallel Relaxation Procedure

```ada
generic
   type Real is digits <>;
   type RealMatrix is array(Integer range <>, Integer range <>)
            of Real;

procedure Parallel_Relaxation(U : in out RealMatrix;
                              MaxErr : in Real;
                              MaxIterations : in Natural;
                              NumberOfRegions : in Natural;
                              DidNotConverge : out Boolean;
                              Omega : in Real := 1.0);

-------------------------------------------------------------------------

with Protected_Counter_Package, Math_Lib, Integer_MaxMin_Lib;
use Integer_MaxMin_Lib;

procedure Parallel_Relaxation(U : in out RealMatrix;
                              MaxErr : in Real;
                              MaxIterations : in Natural;
                              NumberOfRegions : in Natural;
                              DidNotConverge : out Boolean;
                              Omega : in Real := 1.0) is

-- MaxErr determines when we have converged (i.e., we have converged
--    when the change in the value of all points is <= MaxErr).
-- MaxIterations is a limit on how many iterations to perform.  If
--    we perform this many iterations without converging, then we set
--    DidNotConverge to True and return.
-- NumberOfRegions is the maximum number of Ada tasks to use.
-- Omega is the acceleration parameter to the successive overrelaxation
--    formula.

   RowRegions, ColRegions : Integer;
   NumRegions : Integer;
   RowsPerRegion, ColsPerRegion : Integer;
   RowLo : constant Integer := U'FIRST(1);
   RowHi : constant Integer := U'LAST(1);
   ColLo : constant Integer := U'FIRST(2);
   ColHi : constant Integer := U'LAST(2);
   subtype InteriorRows is Integer range RowLo+1..RowHi-1;
   subtype InteriorCols is Integer range ColLo+1..ColHi-1;
   LenInteriorRows : constant Integer := (InteriorRows'LAST -
                                          InteriorRows'FIRST) + 1;

       --    There is no 'LENGTH attribute for discrete
       --    subtypes [§ Appendix A].

   LenInteriorCols : constant Integer := (InteriorCols'LAST -
                                          InteriorCols'FIRST) + 1;
```

```
        package Real_Math_Lib is new Math_Lib(Real);
        use Real_Math_Lib;

        procedure ParRelax_Inner_Proc is separate;

begin

        --    Initially, assume that the system will converge:

        DidNotConverge := False;

        --    See if the matrix U has any interior points. If not, return:

        if U'LENGTH(1) <= 2  or  U'LENGTH(2) <= 2 then
           return;
        end if;

        --    We zero the interior points initially:

        for I in InteriorRows loop
           for J in InteriorCols loop
              U(I, J) := 0.0;
           end loop;
        end loop;

        --    Determine the layout of the regions on the matrix.
        -- Each region is itself a rectangular sub-matrix.  We lay down a
        -- rectangular array of regions on top of the matrix.   The
        -- array is RowRegions by ColRegions:

        RowRegions := Floor(Sqrt(Real(NumberOfRegions)));
        ColRegions := NumberOfRegions / RowRegions;
        NumRegions := RowRegions * ColRegions;

           --  E.g., for NumberOfRegions = 33, we get 5, 6, and 30.
           --  Only the 30 regions are actually used.

        --    Each region is a rectangle of RowsPerRegion rows by
        -- ColsPerRegion columns.  The regions at the right edge
        -- and the bottom may be smaller however:

        RowsPerRegion := (LenInteriorRows + (RowRegions - 1)) / RowRegions;
        ColsPerRegion := (LenInteriorCols + (ColRegions - 1)) / ColRegions;

        --    Now that we know how many tasks we actually want, call
        -- a procedure which declares them & does the relaxation:

        ParRelax_Inner_Proc;

end Parallel_Relaxation;
```

```
------------------------------------------------------------------
--
-- Body of ParRelax_Inner_Proc
--
------------------------------------------------------------------


separate (Parallel_Relaxation)

procedure ParRelax_Inner_Proc is

   task type Region_Task is
      entry SetParameter(SetMyRowRegion,
                         SetMyColRegion : in Integer);
   end Region_Task;

   task type Coordinator_Task is
      entry Wait;
      entry KeepOnGoing;
      entry Finish;
   end Coordinator_Task;

   Regions : array(1..RowRegions, 1..ColRegions) of Region_Task;
   Coordinators : array(1..RowRegions, 1..ColRegions) of
                     Coordinator_Task;
   Unfinished_Counter : Protected_Counter_Package.Protected_Counter;

   task body Coordinator_Task is
      Had_KeepOnGoing: Boolean := False;
      Had_Finish: Boolean := False;
   begin
      loop
         select
            accept KeepOnGoing do
               if not Had_KeepOnGoing then
                  Unfinished_Counter.Incr;
                  Had_KeepOnGoing := True;
               end if;
            end KeepOnGoing;
         or
            when had_KeepOnGoing or Had_Finish =>
               accept Wait do Had_KeepOnGoing := False; end Wait;
         or
            accept Finish do Had_Finish := True; end Finish;
         or
            terminate;
         end select;
      end loop;
   end Coordinator_Task;

   procedure All_Finish is separate;

   task body Region_Task is separate;
```

```
begin      --    The statements of ParRelax_Inner_Proc

   --    The count of unfinished tasks is initially all of the
   -- region tasks:

   Unfinished_Counter.Initialize(NumRegions);

   --    Set the parameters of the regions tasks:

   for I in Regions'RANGE(1) loop
      for J in Regions'RANGE(2) loop
         Regions(I,J).SetParameter(I,J);
      end loop;
   end loop;

-- We now simply wait at the end of the
-- procedure for the tasks to terminate.

end ParRelax_Inner_Proc;
```

```
------------------------------------------------------------------------
--
-- Body of All_Finish Procedure
--
------------------------------------------------------------------------

separate (Parallel_Relaxation.ParRelax_Inner_Proc)

procedure All_Finish is
   -- Calls the Finish entries of all the coordinators.
begin
   for Rreg in Coordinators'RANGE(1) loop
      for Creg in Coordinators'RANGE(2) loop
         Coordinators(Rreg, Creg).Finish;
      end loop;
   end loop;
end All_Finish;

------------------------------------------------------------------------
--
-- Body of Region_Task
--
------------------------------------------------------------------------

separate (Parallel_Relaxation.ParRelax_Inner_Proc)

task body Region_Task is
   MyRowRegion, MyColRegion : Integer;
begin
   --    Task starts by finding out what region it has been
   -- assigned:
   accept SetParameter(SetMyRowRegion, SetMyColRegion : in Integer) do
      MyRowRegion := SetMyRowRegion;
      MyColRegion := SetMyColRegion;
   end;

Region_Inner_Block:

   declare
      MyDone : Boolean;
      New_Value : Real;
      CurCount : Integer;

      --    Compute the boundaries of my region.  These are
      -- the points that will be computed by me:

      MyRowLo : constant Integer := (MyRowRegion - 1) *
                  RowsPerRegion + InteriorRows'FIRST;
      MyColLo : constant Integer := (MyColRegion - 1) *
                  ColsPerRegion + InteriorCols'FIRST;
```

```
          --    If we're at the bottom edge, then MyRowHi should
          -- not exceed InteriorRows'LAST:

          MyRowHi : constant Integer := Min(InteriorRows'LAST,
                    MyRowLo + RowsPerRegion - 1);


          --    Likewise, if we're at the right edge...:

          MyColHi: constant Integer := Min(InteriorCols'LAST,
                    MyColLo + ColsPerRegion - 1);

    begin

    ItersLoop:
       for Iters in 1..MaxIterations loop
          MyDone := True;
          --    Compute a new value for each point in my
          -- region:
          for I in MyRowLo .. MyRowHi loop
             for J in MyColLo .. MyColHi loop
                New_Value := U(I,J) + Omega *
(U(I-1,J) + U(I,J-1) + U(I+1,J) + U(I,J+1) - 4.0*U(I,J)) / 4.0;
                if Abs(New_Value - U(I,J)) >= MaxErr
                   then MyDone := False;
                end if;
                U(i,j) := New_Value;
             end loop; -- over cols
          end loop; --over rows

          if not MyDone then    -- Tell my neighbors to keep on going:
             if MyRowRegion /= 1 then
                Coordinators(MyRowRegion-1,
                            MyColRegion).KeepOnGoing;
             end if;

             if MyRowRegion /= RowRegions then
                Coordinators(MyRowRegion+1,
                            MyColRegion).KeepOnGoing;
             end if;

             if MyColRegion /= 1 then
                Coordinators(MyRowRegion,
                            MyColRegion-1).KeepOnGoing;
             end if;

             if MyColRegion /= ColRegions then
                Coordinators(MyRowRegion,
                            MyColRegion+1).KeepOnGoing;
             end if;
```

```
        else
            Unfinished_Counter.Decr;
            Unfinished_Counter.Read(CurCount);
            if CurCount = 0 then
                --   We're all done.  Wake up
                -- everybody who's sleeping:
                All_Finish;
                goto EndOfTask;
            else
                --   Wait to hear of some change
                -- from my neighbors, or
                -- for all tasks to finish:

                Coordinators(MyRowRegion,
                             MyColRegion).Wait;

                --   We were awakened.  See whether this is
                -- because everybody was finished,
                -- or because of a KeepOnGoing
                -- message:

                Unfinished_Counter.Read(CurCount);
                if CurCount = 0 then
                    goto EndOfTask;
                end if;
            end if;
        end if;

        --   See if some other task has taken too many
        -- iterations already and if so stop iterating:

        exit ItersLoop when DidNotConverge;
    end loop ItersLoop;

    --   Here iff some task (either my task or some
    -- other task) has taken too many iterations:

    DidNotConverge := True;
    All_Finish;
    end Region_Inner_Block;

<<EndOfTask>>
    null;
end Region_Task;
```

6.4 Discussion

6.4.1 Use of Shared Variables

In our solution, we have used the array U as a shared variable. All the region tasks access it directly without any additional protocol. The effects of such simultaneous access to a shared variable are not specified in the Ada language, and will vary from implementation to implementation [§ 9.11]. In some systems, a floating point variable may occupy several bytes of storage, and simultaneous reads and writes may produce an interleaving of bytes: the read may receive some bytes from the value of the variable before the write and some bytes from the value after the write. Thus, the read may receive a value that is neither the previous value of the variable nor the new value. For our solution to be reasonable, we require that the operations of reading and writing the shared variables be indivisible with respect to each other. Note that we do *not* require an indivisible read-modify-write operation.

6.4.2 Updates of Shared Variables From Registers

Another potential difficulty with shared variables is the problem of the compiler keeping such variables in local registers [§ 9.11]. A compiler is required to store these back to the shared variables only at those points where tasks synchronize, e.g., via rendezvous. Fortunately, in our solution we have sufficient synchronization between the region and coordinator tasks for the shared matrix U to be updated when needed. It is thus not necessary for us to employ the predefined generic procedure Shared_Variable_Update [§ 9.11].

6.4.3 Generics and Generic Instantiation

The procedure Parallel_Relaxation is a generic procedure with two generic formal parameters: the floating point data type and a two-dimensional array type of this floating point type [§ 12.1.2]. This allows a user to instantiate the procedure with any floating point data type he has declared. He can, of course, instantiate it several times, for example, once with a floating point type HisShort which is digits 6 and once with a floating point type HisLong which is **digits 12**.

Within the body of the procedure, we need some common mathematical functions on the generic formal type Real (e.g., Floor and Sqrt). Since these are not pre-defined subprograms in the package Standard, we have to arrange for their definition. We assume the existence of a generic library package, Math_Lib, which contains, amongst other facilities, the functions we need. Furthermore, we assume that Math_Lib has one generic formal parameter that is the floating point type for which its facilities are to be provided. We obtain the routines we need by instantiating Math_Lib with our generic parameter Real.

For a subprogram defined in the package Standard as a subprogram for the floating point types (e.g., Abs or "+"), the type Real will automatically inherit the subprogram, via the Ada derived type mechanism [§ 3.4].

6.4.4 Scheduling of Ada Tasks Onto Processors

Our procedure is intended for use with an implementation of Ada on a multiprocessor computer system, that will have some number P of physical processors. Our N Ada tasks will be scheduled onto these processors by the underlying Ada system and/or by the operating system. Of course, we intend that the system will devote more than one processor to our program. However, there is no way of specifying or guaranteeing this within Ada. Suppose that P is less than N, or that the system chooses to give our program less than N dedicated processors, because, for example the system is multi-programmed or time-shared between several independent user programs. Our procedure will nevertheless execute correctly no matter how many processors are running the Ada tasks and no matter what their relative speeds.

Consider the case of having one processor executing our program. Suppose that initially this processor is running some particular region task, A. Since none of this region's neighbors are changing, the region will eventually converge locally. The task A will find the global variable Unfinished_Counter non-zero and will block on the call to its coordinator's Wait entry. Since A is therefore no longer eligible, the processor will find some other eligible Ada task to run. As they block and unblock during rendezvous, our Ada tasks will multiplex themselves onto the single processor.

Observe that this ability to execute correctly on a single processor is a property of our program, and not a general property of any Ada program with multiple Ada tasks. In particular, if a running Ada task never engages in any rendezvous, there is no obligation of the underlying Ada system to ever de-schedule it and let another Ada task execute [§ 9.8].

References

[1]   A.L. Ambler, D.I. Good, J.C. Browne, W.F. Burger, R.M. Cohen, C.G. Hoch and R.E. Wells.
        Gypsy: A Language for Specification and Implementation of Verifiable Programs.
        ACM SIGPLAN Notices 12(3), March, 1977.

[2]   G.M. Baudet.
        Asynchronous Iterative Methods for Multiprocessors.
        Journal of the ACM 25(2):226-244, April, 1978.

[3]   G.M. Baudet.
        The Design and Analysis of Algorithms for Asynchronous Multiprocessors.
        PhD thesis, Dept. of Computer Science, Carnegie-Mellon University, April, 1978.

[4]   J.L. Bentley and M. Shaw.
        An Alphard Specification of a Correct and Efficient Transformation on Data Structures.
        In *Proceedings of IEEE Conference on Specifications of Reliable Software*, pages 222-237.
            IEEE, April, 1979.

[5]   K.L. Bowles.
        Microcomputer Problem Solving Using Pascal.
        Springer-Verlag, 1977.

[6]   P. Brinch Hansen.
        The Programming Language Concurrent Pascal.
        IEEE Transactions on Software Engineering SE-1, June, 1975.

[7]   F.P. Brooks, Jr.
        The Mythical Man-Month: Essays on Software Engineering.
        Addison-Wesley, Reading, Massachusetts, 1975.

[8]   J.C. Browne.
        The Interaction of Operating Systems and Software Engineering.
        Proceedings of the IEEE 68(9), September, 1980.

[9]   J.N. Buxton and B. Randell (editors).
        Software Engineering Techniques.
        NATO, 1970.
        Report on a Conference Sponsored by the NATO Science Committee, Rome, Italy, 27th to 31st
            October 1969.

[10]   O.-J. Dahl.
        Simula 67 Common Base Language.
        Technical Report, Norwegian Computing Center, Oslo, 1968.

[11]   O.-J. Dahl and C.A.R. Hoare.
        Hierarchical Program Structures.
        In *Structured Programming*, pages 175-220. Academic Press, 1972.

[12]   G. Dahlquist and A. Björck.
        Numerical Methods.
        Prentice Hall, Englewood Cliffs, New Jersey, 1974.

[13]   A.M. Davis and T.G. Rauscher.
        Formal Techniques and Automatic Processing to Ensure Correctness in Requirements
            Specifications.
        In *Proceedings of the IEEE Conference on Specifications of Reliable Software*, pages 15-35.
            IEEE Computer Society, 1979.
        IEEE Catalog Number 79 CH1401-9C.

[14]   A.J. Demers and J.E. Donahue.
        Data Types, Parameters and Type Checking.
        In *Proceedings of the ACM Symposium on Principles of Programming Languages*, pages 12-
            23. ACM SIGACT and SIGPLAN, January, 1980.

[15]   Department of Defense.
        Steelman Requirements for High Order Computer Programming Languages.
        1978.

[16]   Department of Defense.
        Reference Manual for the Ada Programming Language.
        November 1980 edition, United States Department of Defense, 1980.

[17]   Department of Defense.
        Requirements for Ada Programming Support Environments: Stoneman.
        1980.

[18]   F. DeRemer and H.H. Kron.
        Programming-in-the-Large vs. Programming-in-the-Small.
        IEEE Transactions on Software Engineering SE-2(2), June, 1976.

[19]   Digital Equipment Corporation.
        PDP-11 Peripherals Handbook.
        Digital Equipment Corporation, Maynard, Massachusetts, 1976.

[20]   Digital Equipment Corporation.
        PDP-11 04/34/45/55 Processor Handbook.
        Digital Equipment Corporation, Maynard, Massachusetts, 1976.

[21]   E.W. Dijkstra.
        Goto Statement Considered Harmful.
        Communications of the ACM 11(3), March, 1968.

[22]   E.W. Dijkstra.
        Notes on Structured Programming.
        In *Structured Programming*, pages 1-82. Academic Press, 1972.

[23]   R. Feiertag and P.G. Neumann.
        The foundations of a provably secure operating system (PSOS).
        In *Proceedings of the National Computer Conference*, pages 329-334. National Computer
            Conference, 1979.

[24]   R.W. Floyd.
        Assigning Meanings to Programs.
        In J.T. Schwartz (editor), *Proceedings of the Symposium in Applied Mathematics*, pages 19-32.
            American Mathematical Society, 1967.

[25]   S.L. Gerhart and L. Yelowitz.
        Observations of Fallibility in Applications of Modern Programming Methodologies.
        IEEE Transactions on Software Engineering SE-2(5), September, 1976.

[26]   S.L. Gerhart and D.S. Wile.
        Preliminary Report on the Delta Experiment: Specification and Verification of a Multiple-User
            File Updating Module.
        In *Proceedings of the IEEE Conference on Specifications of Reliable Software*, pages 198-211.
            IEEE Computer Society, 1979.
        IEEE Catalog Number 79 CH1401-9C.

[27]   C.M. Geschke, J.H. Morris Jr. and E.H. Satterthwaite.
        Early Experience with Mesa.
        Communications of the ACM 20(8), August, 1977.

[28]   J. Goldberg.
        Proceedings of the Symposium on the High Cost of Software.
        Technical Report, Stanford Research Institute, Stanford, California, September, 1973.

[29]   D.I. Good.
        Constructing Verified and Reliable Communications Processing Systems.
        ACM Software Engineering Notes 2(5), October, 1977.

[30]   J.B. Goodenough and C.L. McGowan.
        Software Quality Assurance: Testing and Validation.
        Proceedings of the IEEE 68(9), September, 1980.

[31]   P. Grogono.
        Programming in Pascal.
        Addison-Wesley, Reading, Massachusetts, 1978.

[32]   L.R. Guarino.
        The Evolution of Abstraction in Programming Languages.
        Technical Report CMU-CS-78-120, Carnegie-Mellon University, May, 1978.

[33]   J.V. Guttag.
        Abstract Data Types and the Development of Data Structures.
        Communications of the ACM 20(6), June, 1977.

[34]   J.V. Guttag, E. Horowitz and D.R. Musser.
        Abstract Data Types and Software Validation.
        Communications of the ACM 21(12), December, 1978.

[35]   J.V. Guttag.
        Notes on Type Abstraction (Version 2).
        IEEE Transactions on Software Engineering SE-6(1):13-23, January, 1980.

[36]   J. Guttag and J.J. Horning.
        Formal Specification As a Design Tool.
        In *Proceedings of the ACM Symposium on Principles of Programming Languages*, pages 251-
            261. ACM SIGACT and SIGPLAN, January, 1980.

[37]   K.L. Heninger.
        Specifying Software Requirements for Complex Systems: New Techniques and Their
            Applications.
        In *Proceedings of the IEEE Conference on Specifications of Reliable Software*, pages 1-14.
            IEEE Computer Society, 1979.
        IEEE Catalog Number 79 CH1401-9C.

[38]   P. Hilfinger, G. Feldman, R. Fitzgerald, I. Kimura, R.L. London, K.V.S. Prasad, V.R. Prasad,
        J. Rosenberg, M. Shaw, W.A. Wulf.
        (Preliminary) An Informal Definition of Alphard.
        Research Report CMU-CS-78-105, Carnegie Mellon University, Computer Science Depart-
            ment, February, 1978.

[39]   C.A.R. Hoare.
        An Axiomatic Basis for Computer Programming.
        Communications of the ACM 12, October, 1969.

[40]   C.A.R. Hoare.
        Proof of Correctness of Data Representations.
        Acta Informatica 1(4), 1972.

[41]   C.A.R. Hoare.
        Notes on Data Structuring.
        In *Structured Programming*, pages 83-174. Academic Press, 1972.

[42]   C.A.R. Hoare and N. Wirth.
        An Axiomatic Definition of the Programming Language Pascal.
        Acta Informatica 2(4), 1973.

[43]   E. Horowitz and S. Sahni.
        Fundamentals of Computer Algorithms.
        Computer Science Press, Inc., 1978.

[44]   W.E. Howden.
        An Analysis of Software Validation Techniques for Scientific Programs.
        Technical Report DM-171-IR, University of Victoria Department of Mathematics, March, 1979.

[45]   J.D. Ichbiah, et al.
        Rationale for the Design of the ADA Programming Language.
        ACM SIGPLAN Notices 14(6B), June, 1979.

[46]   *Draft Specification for the Computer Programming Language Pascal.*
        International Organization for Standardization, 1979.
        ISO/TC 97/SC 5 N.

[47]   K. Jensen and N. Wirth.
        Pascal User Manual and Report.
        Springer-Verlag, 1974.

[48]   A.K. Jones and B.H. Liskov.
        An Access Control Facility for Programming Languages.
        MIT Memo 137, Massachusetts Institute of Technology Computation Structures Group and
            Carnegie-Mellon University, 1976.

[49]   B.W. Kernighan and P.J. Plauger.
         Software Tools.
         Addison-Wesley, 1976.

[50]   D.E. Knuth.
         The Art of Computer Programming. Volume 1: *Fundamental Algorithms.*
         Addison-Wesley, 1973.
         Second edition.

[51]   D.E. Knuth.
         The Art of Computer Programming. Volume 2: *Seminumerical Algorithms.*
         Addison-Wesley, 1969.

[52]   D.E. Knuth.
         The Art of Computer Programming. Volume 3: *Sorting and Searching.*
         Addison-Wesley, 1973.

[53]   B.W. Lampson, J.J. Horning, R.L. London, J.G. Mitchell and G.J. Popek.
         Report on the Programming Language Euclid.
         ACM SIGPLAN Notices 12(2), February, 1977.

[54]   B.H. Liskov and S.N. Zilles.
         Specification Techniques for Data Abstractions.
         IEEE Transactions on Software Engineering SE-1, March, 1975.

[55]   B. Liskov, A. Snyder, R. Atkinson and C. Schaffert.
         Abstraction Mechanisms in CLU.
         Communications of the ACM 20(8), August, 1977.

[56]   R.L. London.
         A View of Program Verification.
         In *Proceedings of the International Conference on Reliable Software*, pages 534-545. IEEE
             Computer Society, April, 1975.

[57]   R.L. London, J.V. Guttag, J.J. Horning, B.W. Lampson, J.G. Mitchell and G.J. Popek.
         Proof Rules for the Programming Language Euclid.
         Acta Informatica 10(1):1-26, 1978.

[58]   Z. Manna.
         Mathematical Theory of Computation.
         McGraw-Hill, 1974.

[59]   D.D. McCracken.
         A Guide to Fortran IV Programming, 2nd Edition.
         John Wiley and Sons, New York, 1972.

[60]   J.K. Millen.
         Security Kernel Validation in Practice.
         Communications of the ACM 19(5), May, 1976.

[61]   E. Miller (editor).
         Tutorial: Automated Tools for Software Engineering.
         IEEE Computer Society, 1979.
         IEEE Catalog No. EHO 150-3.

[62]   J.H. Morris.
        Types Are Not Sets.
        In *Proceedings of the ACM Symposium on Principles of Programming Languages*, pages 120-
            124. ACM, 1973.

[63]   J.H. Morris.
        Protection in Programming Languages.
        Communications of the ACM 16, January, 1973.

[64]   P. Naur and B. Randell (editors).
        Software Engineering.
        NATO, 1969.
        Report on a Conference Sponsored by the NATO Science Committee, Garmisch, Germany,
            7th to 11th October 1968.

[65]   A. Newell, F. Tonge, E.A. Feigenbaum, B.F. Green, Jr. and G.H. Mealy.
        Information Processing Language-V Manual.
        Prentice Hall, 1964.

[66]   D.L. Parnas.
        Information Distribution Aspects of Design Methodology.
        In *Proceedings of IFIP Congress*, pages 26-30. IFIP, 1971.
        Booklet TA-3.

[67]   D.L. Parnas.
        A Technique for Software Module Specification with Examples.
        Communications of the ACM 15, May, 1972.

[68]   D.L. Parnas.
        On the Criteria to be Used in Decomposing Systems into Modules.
        Communications of the ACM 15(12), December, 1972.

[69]   L. Peters.
        Software Design Engineering.
        Proceedings of the IEEE 68(9), September, 1980.

[70]   IEEE Computer Society (editor).
        *Workshop on Quantitative Software Models for Reliability, Complexity, and Cost: an Assess-
            ment of the State of the Art*.
        IEEE Computer Society, 1979.
        IEEE Catalog No. TH0067-9.

[71]   L.H. Ramshaw.
        Formalizing the Analysis of Algorithms.
        PhD thesis, Stanford University, 1979.

[72]   S.A. Schuman (editor).
        Proceedings of the International Symposium on Extensible Languages.
        ACM SIGPLAN Notices 6, December, 1971.

[73]   S.A. Schuman.
        On Generic Functions.
        In *New Directions in Algorithmic Languages -- 1975*, pages 169-192. IRIA, 1976.

[74] M. Shaw, W.A. Wulf and R.L. London.
Abstraction and Verification in Alphard: Defining and Specifying Iteration and Generators.
Communications of the ACM 20(8), August, 1977.

[75] M. Shaw, G. Feldman, R. Fitzgerald, P. Hilfinger, I. Kimura, R. London, J. Rosenberg and W.A. Wulf.
Validating the Utility of Abstraction Techniques.
In *Proceedings of ACM National Conference*, pages 106-110. ACM, December, 1978.

[76] M. Shaw.
A Formal System for Specifying and Verifying Program Performance.
Technical Report CMU-CS-79-129, Carnegie-Mellon University, June, 1979.

[77] M. Shaw and W.A. Wulf.
Toward Relaxing Assumptions in Languages and Their Implementations.
SIGPLAN Notices 13(3):45-61, March, 1980.

[78] M. Sherman and M. Borkan.
A Flexible Semantic Analyzer for Ada.
In *Symposium on the Ada Programming Language*. ACM, Boston, December, 1980.

[79] IEEE Computer Society (editor).
Proceedings of the Conference on Specifications of Reliable Software.
IEEE Computer Society, 5855 Naples Plaza, Suite 301, Long Beach, California 90803, 1979.
IEEE Catalog No. 79 CH1401-9C.

[80] T.A. Standish.
A Data Definition Facility for Programming Languages.
PhD thesis, Carnegie-Mellon University, Department of Computer Science, 1967.

[81] R.J. Swan, S.H. Fuller and D.P. Siewiorek.
Cm*: A Modular, Multi-Microprocessor.
In *Proc. 1977 National Computer Conference*. American Federation of Information Processing Societies, 1977.

[82] B.J. Walker, R.A. Kemmerer and G.J. Popek.
Specification and Verificaton of the UCLA Security Kernel.
Communications of the ACM 23(2), February, 1980.

[83] J.H. Wensley, L. Lamport, M.W. Green, K.N. Levitt, P.M. Melliar-Smith, R.E. Shostak and C.B. Weinstock.
SIFT: Design and Analysis of a Fault-tolerant Computer for Aircraft Control.
Proceedings of the IEEE 66(10):1240-1255, October, 1978.

[84] N. Wirth.
Program Development by Stepwise Refinement.
Communications of the ACM 14(4), April, 1971.

[85] N. Wirth.
Modula: A Language for Modular Programming.
Software — Practice and Experience 7(1), January, 1977.

[86] W.A. Wulf and M. Shaw.
Global Variables Considered Harmful.
ACM SIGPLAN Notices 8, February, 1973.

[87]   W.A. Wulf, R.L. London and M. Shaw.
        An Introduction to the Construction and Verification of Alphard Programs.
        IEEE Transactions on Software Engineering SE-2(4), December, 1976.

[88]   W.A. Wulf, M. Shaw, P.N. Hilfinger and L. Flon.
        Fundamental Structures of Computer Science.
        Addison-Wesley, 1981.

[89]   W.A. Wulf and C.G. Bell.
        C.mmp - A Multi-Mini-Processor.
        In *Proc. 1972 Fall Joint Computer Conference.* American Federation of Information
            Processing Societies, 1972.

[90]   R.T. Yeh and P. Zave.
        Specifying Software Requirements.
        Proceedings of the IEEE 68(9), September, 1980.